HOW TO ORGANIZE
THE NEIGHBORHOOD
FOR DELINQUENCY PREVENTION

HOW TO ORGANIZE THE NEIGHBORHOOD FOR DELINQUENCY PREVENTION

Anthony Sorrentino

DePaul University
Chicago, Illinois

Copyright © 1979 by Human Sciences Press
72 Fifth Avenue, New York, New York 10011

Printed in the United States of America
9 987654321

Library of Congress Cataloging in Publication Data

Sorrentino, Anthony
  How to organize the neighborhood for delinquency prevention.

  Bibliography: p.
  Includes index.
  1. Juvenile corrections. 2. Community-based corrections. 3. Juvenile delinquency—Prevention. I. Title.
HV9069.S77   364.4   LC 79-1279
ISBN 0-87705-391-X

To Clifford R. Shaw and Henry D. McKay

CONTENTS

7

108756

PREFACE

In view of the present crisis of apparently rising juvenile crime rates, at least two broad alternatives open up before us. Many people favor "getting tough with young criminals." Recommendations are made to give longer sentences to juvenile offenders: this would have the effect of isolating, for even longer periods of time, kids who have committed crimes with other kids who have committed crimes, an obviously unwise course of action.

The model of stricter punishment appears to be an application of what some people believe to be sound child-care practices in the home to an institutional setting. Whatever their results in the context of the family, uncritically transferring those practices into a system of juvenile justice is fraught with danger. If juvenile institutions were the paradises of "correction" that some people, in their ignorance, like to think they are, all would be well. But people familiar with governmental institutions of any sort are not so naive. The failure of correctional facilities to "rehabilitate" youths or adults is well known.

Keeping a youth in such an institution for a longer period of time will more likely make him or her more thoroughly socialized in criminal behavior than would have happened during a shorter period or in no time spent in an institution.

An alternative to this is to do our work of prevention and rehabilitation in the neighborhood where the child lives in the first place. After all, unless the state keeps the offender incarcerated for the rest of that person's young *and adult* life, it is to that same area that he or she will almost certainly return upon leaving the institution. If no change has occurred *inside* the person and no change has taken place in the *external* environment the individual returns to, everything will pick up where it was before: business as usual.

Viewing state correctional institutions on one hand and local neighborhood areas on the other, some latter-day Brigham Young of juvenile justice would have to say: "This is the place," pointing to the places where people live, work, and play, and turning away from the places where people are forced to stay for awhile against their will. In fact, community-based programs of delinquency prevention are beginning to attract a following today as never before. They are not a magical panacea, but they are intelligent uses of resources.

Students of community organization in recent years have raised some searching questions about the Shaw-McKay model, presented in this volume. They have pointed out, for example, that the target area of a neighborhood organization of the type described in these pages is often powerless to deal with the root causes of delinquency or to have any significant impact on the social, economic, and political conditions that usually transcend the neighborhood. It has been proposed, instead, that large-scale, multiissue community organizations encompassing a larger geographical area are needed to deal with larger issues. In some cases, community organizers have created coalitions of special interest groups on a citywide basis.

Perhaps the best example of the latter model of community organization is exemplified by Saul Alinsky's Industrial Areas Foundation. Although Alinsky was on Shaw's staff at the Institute for Juvenile Research in the 1930s, and organized the Back of the Yards Neighborhood Council as the first of many large communitywide organizations, he also utilized some of Shaw's basic ideas, especially the concept of the "indigenous worker." However, the differences were enormous. Essentially Shaw believed in working "within the system" although he urged and hoped that community committees would confront the power structure when necessary. On the other hand, Alinsky organized people to amass power to oppose institutions within and outside the community. While both Shaw and Alinsky agreed on the need for power on the part of people residing in delinquency areas, their strategies were quite different. To Shaw power was to be used to remedy one or another community problem by attracting resources or concessions from the powerful. Alinsky, militant and radical in his approach, used the power of people representing churches, labor unions, and other institutions in the community to fight basic injustices by attacking the oppressors.

In a recent self-study with the aid of outside consultants, the Chicago Area Project came to the conclusion that this conflict between two theories of community organizing need no longer exist. In practice the two are complementary, and the key to understanding lies in an understanding of the appropriate unit for both. In Chicago, for example, both types of community organization coexist, with interesting variations in program content. The Alinsky model tends to focus on broad social, economic, and political problems and issues of a relatively large community area with a population of over 100,000; the Shaw-Area Project model utilizes the neighborhood as the unit of operation usually covering a smaller geographic area of approximately 10,000 to 20,000 people. The former prefers a strategy of conflict, while the latter respects the power of consent and growth in individuals and operates in a spirit of cooperation.

Considering our rapidly changing society, grappling as it is with a multitude of social ills, both approaches appear to have a place in today's world.

The rationality of such programs is increased when researchers use the experience of similar programs that have already been tried. This book is a compilation of some of the assumptions and methods that have been employed for over 40 years, making this program the nation's oldest community-based program of delinquency prevention. Indeed, this book is used as a training manual for community workers in the Illinois Commission on Delinquency Prevention. As such it could be read with profit by organizers of and workers in similar delinquency prevention programs everywhere.

In any community-based effort, no one is an island. I am indebted to many colleagues for making this book possible. My greatest debt is to Clifford R. Shaw and Henry D. McKay, whose studies at the Institute for Juvenile Research in Chicago made a valuable contribution to the understanding of delinquency. Since I was in touch with their thinking and writing for many years on a daily basis, it is basically their ideas and methods that are represented here. In addition, in some places I have used reports, position papers, and other data compiled by Shaw and McKay and other colleagues.

I have drawn some material from an unpublished staff manual edited by Walter Klimek, Commissioner of the now-defunct Illinois Youth Commission, based on field reports from staff members. Staff who have made major contributions are Ray Raymond, Daniel Brindisi, Russ Anderson, Joseph Giunta, Alex Coutts, Mrs. Sadie Jones, Ann Hamilton, Henry Martinez, E. Toy Fletcher, Joseph Loscuito, Alexander McDade, John Giampa, John Harris, Alonzo Scott, Eugene Wroblewski and Emil Peluso.

I have also drawn from other published writings of mine (see the Bibliography). James Bennett has worked on editing the manuscript. All of these people have strengthened this book; my sincere thanks go to them for their help.

I particularly thank Peter Hunt, Executive Director of the Chicago Area Project, and the entire board of directors for their assistance toward publication.

Anthony Sorrentino

Chapter 1

DELINQUENCY AND NEIGHBORHOOD ORGANIZATION

All of us are aware of the continuing seriousness and complexity of the problem of delinquency—especially in the inner-city areas. Indeed, today there are few neighborhoods, even in suburbia, that are not confronted with problems of juvenile antisocial behavior. The rapidly changing character of today's neighborhood, influenced in part by easy mobility, has made it almost impossible to create the community spirit of the "good old days" in which the family, school, church, and other institutions joined forces to set socially approved standards of behavior that youth were also expected to follow.

While the inner-city areas have been undergoing rapid social changes for many decades, there is evidence that these changes have been proceeding at a greater rate during the past two decades, resulting in greater instability and the disruption of social life and interpersonal relationships.

Today, however, it is a different story. Migration into the city, almost at a standstill during the 1930s and 1940s has since accelerated to such a rate as to practically disorganize communities overnight. Well-established communities are fast disappearing and children throughout the city are growing up amid conflicting cultures and behavior norms. The feeling of belonging, of recognition and security, and the desire for common action and neighborliness has crumbled in the face of the invasion of newcomers who are seeking greater economic opportunities of the big city, and who, in many cases, are ill prepared for anonymous city life.

The outlying communities in the city as well as suburbia are also affected by the changes now taking place in the inner-city areas. The original residents of the older neighborhoods eagerly seek new homes in the outlying city and suburban areas. As a result, population in these new communities has doubled, and tripled in some, within a very short period of time, making it most difficult for the orderly assimilation of the incoming familes, and establishment of any sense of "community."

SOCIAL CHANGES

Never before in human history have there been so many technological innovations affecting our daily lives—the increased use of the automobile, which contributes so much to mobility of the population including teenagers; the ready access to air travel; and automation in factories and offices, bringing new designs, processes, and procedures in manufacturing and business—that have all created joblessness on one hand and many new technical opportunities on the other. No longer is there a reservoir of work opportunities for the untrained and uneducated.

The job of "laborer" is fast disappearing. These changes have had a significant impact on everyone—especially on young people without education and training. Many persons, unable to compete in this fast-moving new world of industry and business, feel insecure and thus are unable to deal adequately with their everyday problems of earning a living and providing food for the table.

These changes in our national economic and social order are further complicated by unsettled world conditions and competition between the major powers. The threat of atomic warfare and its resulting disruption of our lives has had a direct effect on the ideals and goals of young people, which contributes to general uncertainty and insecurity. In view of all this, it is no wonder that we are confronted with tremendous problems of delinquent behavior among children and youth of the nation, especially in the congested urban areas.

Recent studies of community areas in Chicago and other cities reveal that certain areas of a big city produce a disproportionate share of juvenile delinquency (Shaw & McKay, 1969). This is not a new phenomenon but has been true for generations. These areas are located around the Loop (Chicago) or central business district, and adjacent to industrial areas. We call them "delinquency" or inner-city areas. They are the neighborhoods where migrant groups, new to the city, first settle. As they prosper and climb the socioeconomic ladder they move away, and are replaced by successive waves of other migrants.

SUCCESSION OF ETHNIC AND RACIAL GROUPS

During the early years of this century these areas were occupied successively by various European immigrant groups who held the least desirable status—economically, socially, and politically. Neighborhood institutions, so important in the development of community morals and controls, were limited to those associated with religious groups and mutual aid and were only moderately successful in meeting the needs of the new generation.

These areas are currently occupied by new migrant groups, many of them from the depressed areas of the United States and its territories. In spite of the changing picture of these areas, by entry of people of different ethnic origins, patterns of delinquency have remained basically the same. As in other phases of human culture, these are passed on from youth to youth and from gang to gang in these neighborhoods. This delinquent world provides the same sanctions, awards, and approvals for the delinquent that conventional society provides for the nondelinquent.

Today, the problem of juvenile delinquency is beginning to spill over into many neighborhoods, which, 10 years ago, were quite stable. As the waves of new migrants move into the city, more and more neighborhoods succumb to the resulting changes. Many absentee property owners, seeing opportunities for excess profits, cut up large apartments into smaller units and reduce maintenance. As a result, the physical condition of these properties deteriorates causing further decay of these communities and general demoralization of the newcomers. Furthermore, many of the established institutions that lent stability to these communities have become weak and inadequate in meeting the needs of their residents. Others have closed their doors and left. As a result, juveniles have no local haven or hangout where they can spend their spare time and energies. In addition, police contacts, school truancy, and vandalism among juveniles show marked increases.

CLIFFORD SHAW'S STUDIES

The late Clifford R. Shaw and his associates at the Institute for Juvenile Research in Chicago have studied the concentration of delinquents in relation to the city as a whole. They observed and evaluated the social experiences of the delinquent in his or her play group, family, and neighborhood. From these studies, they concluded that delinquent behavior is *acquired,* that it is a product of the social experience of the youngster. Furthermore, they recognized that high delinquency rate areas generally are characterized by confused standards, weak conventional institutions, traditions of delinquency and crime, and a general indifference on the part of the residents to the problem of delinquency and crime.

Another important point drawn from Shaw's studies is that when youth—especially adolescent males—become excluded from conventional society, they tend to form subcultural groups in their effort to find support and approval for their behavior. This exclusion from conventional institutions becomes a most important factor in communities where delinquent patterns prevail. Street-corner society then sets the patterns of life for many of the potential delinquents, providing opportunities for growing youngsters to find and achieve their status as human beings. Excluded from many of the conventional groups, the youngster engages in delinquent activity and turns to the only social groupings available to him or her (McKay, 1962). If we view delinquent behavior in this way, we realize that the youth in trouble is not necessarily antisocial, destructive, and cruel by nature, but is a growing youngster with the same needs and aspirations as other youngsters have.

From all of this it becomes quite clear that the neighborhood—its residents and their expressed attitudes, behavior patterns, and cultural norms—molds the life of the growing youngster. If juvenile delinquency becomes a problem to the neighborhood, the answer lies within the residents and the institutions of the community (Short, 1976).

IMPORTANCE OF NEIGHBORHOOD APPROACH

Clifford Shaw believed that the neighborhood must be made aware that delinquency is a product of neighborhood life, and that effective prevention and treatment demands a dynamic, positive action program, which can be accomplished best through the coordinated efforts of all the residents, that is, through community organization.

Community organization does not come easily. The organizers must work diligently, literally "selling" the needs for neighborhood action door to door. Leaflets and brochures are helpful. Searching for leadership to guide the program, the organizers will not stop with the known leaders of the community, but will seek to uncover latent talents and ability among people at all levels. Much talent for a neighborhood self-help program will be found among the butcher, the baker, and the candlestick maker—carpenters, plumbers, engineers, bricklayers, and schoolteachers—indeed, anyone with an interest in the problem and a sincere desire to help.

Community organization work in Chicago and in over 100 other towns and cities in Illinois, has taken the form of committees developed within small neighborhoods (Sorrentino, 1959). "Community organization" is referred to here as a process, encompassing the procedures, techniques, and strategies used in formulating, planning, and implementing social welfare programs. The neighborhood, usually a smaller and cohesive geographic unit than a community, is proposed here as the unit of operation for the reasons discussed above.

We consider the neighborhood as a small area in which the population has certain predominating characteristics—a similarity in educational, social, and economic levels, or in religion, race, or nationality. A strong common bond results in easier community organization because the goals and program operation are more easily understood.

Many people will raise the question as to what ordinary residents can do to reduce or control delinquency. They feel, perhaps, that this is a job for the experts or the professionals. While no one can deny the importance of having the technical assistance of professionally trained staff in working with the delinquent or potential delinquent, the significance of resident participation in this program is unquestionable. Only through the concerted action of the residents is it possible to surround the growing child with a set of conventional moral values. To be effective, these values must be provided by the people who live near the youngsters and who can influence them from day to day (Sorrentino, 1977).

There are many things an organization of local residents can do. (1) It can serve as an action group to eliminate influences contributing to delinquency in the community. (2) It can provide constructive relationships for the delinquent or potential delinquent. (3) It can provide for better use of existing welfare services in the community—both public and private—and support the need for additional resources and services (Finestone, 1976).

ACTIVITIES OF NEIGHBORHOOD ORGANIZATIONS

A neighborhood organization interested in providing services for the treatment of the delinquent can sponsor group activities for the young people of the community and encourage all youth to participate. The committee can provide individual counseling for youth with problems, assist in job finding, or help them meet their school problems. They might raise funds to provide other resources and services when required. Moreover, a committee can, through group action, mobilize sentiment against unprincipled persons who exploit young people; it can bring pressure to bear on local businesses that sell liquor or pornographic literature to minors; it can identify and report adults who purchase stolen merchandise, especially if they involve youngsters in their activity. These and many other similar conditions to be found in inner-city areas or any neighborhood undergoing major social changes can be effectively dealt with by an organization of residents banded together as a youth or community committee. Many organizations established in Chicago often call themselves civic or community committees, but in reality they are neighborhood groups and their target population is within the confines of a neighborhood area.

Many of the committees sponsor a wide variety of programs. Some committees sponsor youth clubs in neighborhoods where there is a lack of recreational facilities. Such committees, however, are urged not to compete with other local recreation agencies but, instead, to cooperate with them, striving for better use of the facilities and helping to improve the existing services.

Other committees have helped to build, equip, and maintain playgrounds for neighborhood children. Two committees in the Chicago area operate their own summer camps, completely built through the efforts of volunteers.

Committees can present a statement of their community needs to the city or state officials, and, as a group of voting citizens, press for the needed additional services. These services might range from improving school and recreational services to providing better garbage collections, repairing and maintaining streets, or installing traffic lights at dangerous intersections.

There are many other activities in which committees engage, depending largely on the needs of the particular neighborhood. Some of the committees have been instrumental in developing community renewal programs; others have emphasized social welfare referral services. The philosophy underlying all of the programs of the committees, however, is the same: the desire to create and develop opportunities for the prevention of delinquency, and to treat young people who have been adjudged delinquent. For only through joint efforts of the neighborhood to the young offender can rehabilitation be complete—and without rehabilitation, no program for the prevention of juvenile delinquency can be truly effective.

HUMAN RESOURCES

Programs of neighborhood organization in Illinois and elsewhere have demonstrated that untapped human resources are available and can be utilized for youth welfare and delinquency prevention. Through the instrumentality of a citizens' group, persons not ordinarily involved in welfare work can be given meaningful roles. Moreover, such self-help neighborhood organizations encourage wider participation in democratic social action programs. Without question, many activities directed toward the improvement of local communities have grown out of these efforts. New leadership and talent have been discovered for community welfare programs, new financial resources have been uncovered, and new ways of making use of existing institutions have been developed. Every community can identify and utilize these new sources of community strengths advantageously in its efforts to prevent delinquency and to help young people become productive citizens.

The late Dr. Ernest W. Burgess, eminent sociologist of the University of Chicago, teacher of Clifford Shaw, and cofounder of the Chicago Area Project, stated:

> If juvenile delinquency is essentially a manifestation of neighborhood disorganization, then evidently only a program of neighborhood organization can cope with it and control it . . . [there] . . . can be no substitute for a group of leading citizens of a neighborhood who take the responsibility of a program for delinquency treatment and prevention . . .
>
> If we wish to reduce delinquency, we must radically change our thinking about it. We must think of its causes more in terms of the community and less in terms of the individual. We must plan our programs with emphasis upon social rather than upon individual factors in delinquency . . .
>
> We must realize that the brightest hope in reformation is in changing the neighborhood and in control of the gang in which the boy lives, and has his being and to which he returns after institutional treatment. And, finally, we must reaffirm our faith in prevention, which is so much easier, cheaper, and more effective than cure and which begins with the home, the play group, the local school, the church, and the neighborhood (Burgess, 1975).

DIVERTING CHILDREN FROM THE CRIMINAL JUSTICE SYSTEM

Largely due to the influence of Clifford Shaw, Ernest Burgess, and other sociologists, the emphasis today in the entire juvenile and adult criminal justice system is on alternatives to commitment to institutions. The local community today is shown to be the most responsible and logical agent for preventing children from becoming involved in the criminal justice system. The public is beginning to see that correctional institutions have not been very successful in rehabilitating offenders. Follow-up studies, based on official records, show that two-thirds to three-fourths of delinquents dealt with by such agencies have continued in delinquency despite a wide variety of treatment methods (McKay, 1967). At the same time, the costs to the taxpayer have been astronomical. In Illinois the average per capita cost in a juvenile institution is estimated to run between $15,000 and $20,000; in New York State, between $16,000 and $24,000 annually. The U.S. average is between $8,000 and $12,000 (the best private school at college level doesn't begin to cost this much).

Perhaps part of the reasons for the failures encountered are due to forces inherent in society. Delinquency and crime are essentially products of social change, which brings about disruption and instability in community life. No one knows how to deal adequately with such complex social influences. All societies undergoing rapid change are therefore going to pay the price of high delinquency and crime rates. In such situations, the socialization process breaks down, especially for the adolescent in disadvantaged areas. All too often there are few paths to legitimate activity, and, as a result, the adolescent is locked into roles of passivity and powerlessness. Mental illness, drug use, delinquency, and the rackets thus often become the only outlets, the only way out of the social jungles in which young people live.

What do we do with the offender? Society must act to preserve its values, define norm-violating behavior, and set limits to what it will or will not tolerate. Society therefore does act toward the delinquent, usually negatively and hostilely: it labels, stigmatizes, and brands him or her as an outcast. The offender is removed, cast out of conventional society. He or she is processed through the juvenile justice system, which further alienates him or her from conventional society. This is the dilemma: how to act against the offender without causing damage and complicating his or her problem? There are no easy answers.

For those youngsters who must be removed to protect them and the community, the state must provide good, decent care and custody. It is a myth to postulate the idea, as we have over the years, that we will "treat" and "correct" the offenders. Institutions by their very nature cannot correct. And exactly what are they supposed to correct? This approach assumes that the offender is sick or pathological when actually it is the community—society—that is sick and should be regarded as the patient. We have given unrealistic, if not impossible, tasks to custodial institutions. And in the process we have fooled the public and placed heavy burdens and frustrations on institutional personnel.

The trend toward alternatives to commitment is in the right direction. By continuing to reduce commitments, emphasis can be placed on smaller, community-based group homes and intervention strategies utilizing community organization approaches, youth service bureaus, programs of youth involvement, and support to social action measures to improve housing, health, employment, and other services to disadvantaged communities.

The President's Commission on Crime and Law Enforcement advocated action along these lines, among many others, but implementation has been slow. Administrators should clearly give priority to social measures designed to deal with the roots of the problem in the community. A much greater investment is needed to provide more resources to carry on various types of community programs to divert children away from the juvenile justice system.

The neighborhood and community projects, based on the pioneer work of the Chicago Area Project, is one model (Sorrentino, 1959, 1975). The development of local youth commissions and township committees on youth in suburban areas is another. A variety of youth and community councils are also based on similar methods.

The author's conviction and basic philosophy is that it is indispensable in all such efforts that we utilize the human resources to be found in the neighborhood—local residents and indigenous leaders, organized into self-help, self-governing enterprises, working cooperatively with all the institutions in the community.

Chapter 2

THE COMMUNITY-BASED
APPROACH

In recent years, invaluable scientific data have been accumulated on social forces in the community. The most direct application of these data to treatment of social problems has been made in such fields as progressive education, group work, social work, public health, the indigenous church movement, and adult education.

In progressive education, emphasis has been placed on such principles as (1) the integration of agencies dealing with the child and (2) the community approach that avoids paternalism, routinization, and authoritarianism that would hinder, if not block, free group development.

In group work, these principles have come to the fore and have been made the basis for a new attack on community disorganization (Coyle, 1938). In this field, there has been general agreement on the principles of (1) an educational process beginning with the community, (2) experimentation in social action—"the use of social materials, just as we use other materials, for program purposes," and (3) providing opportunities for participation at the level of understanding and acceptance of the community. These principles are dramatically illustrated in Isabel Merritt's "Up from Charity," a description of Stryker's Lane in New York City (Merritt, 1938):

> So runs the story of Stryker's Lane. In 1927 a neighborhood suspicious and baffled, antagonistic to suggestion from outside, and torn by internal discord. In 1938, a neighborhood functioning through a central organization of its own creation, self-governed and self-supported to an amazing degree, and co-operating with outside groups in civic, health, social, and recreational programs.
>
> Such is the change. What is the clue? It is the belief of Stryker's Lane that self-creation, self-direction, and self-support are the dynamos of social progress and that philanthropy with its boards of directors and staffs should not overlook these generators of energy. . . . When the people were given opportunity to do what they wanted to do, in their own way, and at their own pace . . . forces either dormant or perverted were released and redirected to rescue a baffled neighborhood.

Many more citations of a similar nature from the literature in the field of group work might be made. Charles E. Hendry (1939), speaking from the viewpoint of the national boys' work movement emphasizes the importance of this community approach, especially with respect to the use of natural leaders:

> Until and unless we are prepared to enlist the residents of neighborhoods and their leaders, and to entrust them with a share in the responsibilities and privileges of administration, we fail to operate as becomes an agency in a democracy.

The merits of enlisting leadership and participation on a neighborhood basis have been most dramatically demonstrated in the field of public health. The fashion in which the Rockefeller Foundation has operated through forces indigenous to the community is brought out in Victor Heiser's story of his experience as Director of the International Health Board of the Rockefeller Foundation. The Foundation knew at the outset of their work in the South that it would be necessary to operate through the local health agencies already existing, since jealousy of "Northern philanthropic invasion" would stop the project before it was well under way. Their aim was to build up local departments so that these might in time function by themselves. Victor Heiser (1936) writes:

> We always had to bear in mind that we have to have public opinion on our side. Public opinion conceives of sanitation in terms of collecting garbage and cleaning dirty streets, removing dead animals, cutting weeds and grass on vacant lots, keeping goats out of back alleys, sweeping sidewalks, penning up pigs, and deodorizing foul smells. We had to do all the things which the public regarded as most important, even to seeing that their whiskey was free of impurities.
>
> One of the hardest abnegations was entailed by our stipulation that the local health organization should receive credit for whatever success might be accomplished.
>
> As a rule our men were never heard of in the outside world. Scientists usually want the fruits of their labor in the shape of public recognition, but we could not allow this. I sympathized deeply, but could do nothing save encourage them in their work.

Well-known studies of the foreign missionary movement have all pointed out the importance of the indigenous church program in foreign missionary work. The chief characteristics of this movement were its emphasis on the use of local leaders, the recognition and respect for native culture, and the use of the missionary as a friend and counselor in programs for local welfare.

Adult education programs are based on principles of democratic participation in group life, effective social organization through actual training, and practice in the technologies of good citizenship. Mere knowledge of facts, it is agreed, is not enough.

These movements toward educating the public regarding its responsibility for its own welfare are based on understanding the futility of merely perfecting the technical methods of the past and repeating historical mistakes, and realizing the need for experimentation.

LIMITATION OF CURRENT PRACTICES IN PREVENTION AND TREATMENT OF DELINQUENCY

Despite efforts at suppression of crime in recent decades, the volume of delinquency has not decreased in the deteriorated urban areas.[1]

It has long been recognized that correctional schools, reformatories, and prisons, while necessary for the immediate protection of life and property, are not effective in aiding offend-

---

[1]The inadequacy of probation, incarceration and parole in the treatment of juvenile offenders residing in the delinquency areas of Chicago is illustrated by a case study that has been carried on by the Department of Sociology at the Institute for Juvenile Research since 1922. The case in question is that of an immigrant family in which the five brothers all became involved in delinquency at the early age of 6 years and continued in delinquent and criminal practices throughout a period of 15 years or more. All of these brothers were repeatedly placed on probation in the Chicago Parental School, the Chicago Cook County School and the State Industrial School at St. Charles, and four of them have been incarcerated in reformatories and prisons. The combined total of their periods of incarceration in correctional institutions, reformatories and prisons is now approximately 55 years, although the oldest brother is now only 33. This incarceration entailed an expenditure in public funds of more than $30,000, not to mention the cost of probation, parole, property damage, and the rather continuous service rendered by a family case-work agency during a period of more than 20 years. See Clifford R. Shaw citation in bibliography.

ers to become law-abiding citizens. As early as 1837, John Clay, an English authority on criminology, made the following significant observations that might well have been written today:

> It was once a truth so fully recognized as to become proverbial that "a criminal came out of prison worse than when he went in." To the young criminal the proverb bore a special application. His vicious education, begun in parental poverty, or neglect, or bad example, was completed in Gaol. . . .

Archibald Allison (1840) reaffirmed this observation:

> In the course of nearly twenty years of official connection with this subject, the author has witnessed the progress of many thousand persons upon whom short imprisonments have produced no other effect than that of preparing them for long ones, and the long ones of rendering them ripe for transportation.

These early observations to the effect that incarceration tends to confirm the inmate in his or her criminality have been given added support in recent years by systematic studies of prison life and of the careers of offenders subsequent to their release from penal institutions. A large proportion of boys in the Boston Juvenile Court subsequently were found to be engaged in delinquency (Glueck & Glueck, 1934). Studies in Chicago by Shaw and associates have corroborated this and showed that the greatest proportion of boys who continued in delinquency were those who resided in delinquency areas of the city.

Inasmuch as these traditional methods of dealing with delinquency and crime have not yielded the desired results, it is apparent that new procedures must be discovered. From the studies referred to above, and from many others that exist, it appears that much of the delinquency in blighted areas is conduct molded by community forces that are integrally related to the whole social world in which the individual is immersed. If this assumption is valid, it follows that procedures for the prevention and treatment of delinquency in those areas should be sufficiently comprehensive to include programs of community reorganization and to supplement techniques of individual care for medical, psychiatric, and family case work agencies.

There seems to be no correlation between the number of group work agencies in deteriorated areas and the volume of delinquency and crime. Certain areas that have been studied intensively by the Institute for Juvenile Research for the last 40 years have shown a uniformly high rate of delinquency despite the fact that the number of such agencies in these areas has been considerably increased during the same period of time.

That such agencies render invaluable service to Chicago as a whole and to the welfare of the persons in the local neighborhoods who participate in their programs is unquestioned. There seems to be considerable factual evidence, however, that many of these agencies, at least as they are operated at the present time, are not adequately providing for the needs of the delinquent child. Some of the limitations of character-building institutions in coping with delinquency were suggested by W. I. Thomas and F. Znaniecki (1927) over 40 years ago in their studies of the Polish peasant in America:

> It is a mistake to suppose that a "community center" established by American social agencies can in its present form even approximately fulfill the social function of a Polish parish. It is an institution imposed from the outside instead of being freely developed by the initiative and cooperation of the people themselves and this, in addition to its racially unfamiliar character, would be enough to prevent it from exercising any deep social influence. Its managers usually know little or nothing of the traditions, attitudes and native language of the people with whom they have to deal, and therefore could not become genuine social leaders under any conditions. The institution is based on the type of a "club" which is entirely unknown to the Polish peasant. Whatever common activities it tried to develop are almost exclusively "leisure time" activities; and while these undoubtedly do correspond to a real social need, they are not sufficient by themselves to keep a community together and

should be treated only as a desirable super-structure to be raised upon a foundation of *economic* co-operation. Whatever real assistance the American social center gives to the immigrant community is the result of the "case method" which consists in dealing directly and separately with individuals or families. While this method may bring efficient temporary help to the individual it does not contribute to the social progress of the community nor does it possess much preventive influence in struggling against social disorganization. Both these purposes can be attained only by organizing and encouraging social self-help on the co-operative basis. . . .

Presumably the function of neighborhood insitutions is to foster among the residents a spirit of *responsibility, independence,* and *self-reliance,* in coping with their community problems. The social agency can in this sense make one of its chief contributions by encouraging expression of the community's native leadership. The ideal situation would be one in which the interests of the community were served by only one leadership, in which the objectives of the social service agencies and the aims and aspirations of the community were merged in common effort for the promotion of the welfare of the community. C. C. North (1931) stated that a significant social agency should represent the interests and thoughts of the community.

In the effort to establish a division of field among social agencies operating within a given area, there is a strong tendency to apportion segments of the community among the agencies as "spheres of interest." Although this practice may be necessary and helpful as an administrative device, there is a real danger that the agency may fail to establish a dynamic relationship with the local community and think of its task as something apart from the real interests of the people it seeks to serve.

Caroline Ware, in her study of social welfare work in Greenwich Village in New York City (1935), notes a spirit of proprietorship on the part of many social agencies:

In the face of feeling of those who conducted various social work activities that they "possessed" THE district, it required a positive effort to see the community as something other than so many clients or patients or members of this or that agency—so many people to be adjusted, innoculated, recreated, or what-have-you. When the present study was undertaken, every effort was made to avoid approaching the community through social channels, in order better to see it in its own terms. The ubiquity of the social agencies made it very difficult to carry out this effort.

The institution's conception of its role and function is often quite different from the conception assigned to it by the local community. These facilities of the institution that can be utilized inside the community's own universe of values—as, for example, the game room, gymnasium, and swimming pool—may frequently be regarded as convenient luxuries. The conventional institution may, in a sense, become an object to be exploited. This approach may lead to a very definite type of selectivity in clientele. Such a selectivity may operate not only from the point of view of the institution but also from the viewpoint of the persons it seeks to serve. More often than not, then, the predelinquent and delinquent groups would not share in it, finding other personal contacts and spontaneous activities in the community more engrossing. Even though many delinquents may participate in the programs of these agencies for a time, the period of their membership is usually of short duration.

THE IMPORTANCE OF NATURAL GROUPS AND NATURAL LEADERS

In every community there may be found distinct hierarchies and wide varieties of social groupings based on mutual interests that serve as a means of satisfying certain needs and purposes that the members of the community possess in common. Among these are churches, clubs, societies, lodges, and play groups. For the most part, these are *natural social* groupings indigenous to the life of the community and sustained by the initiative and effort of their own members. Along with the family, they exert the forces that contribute largely to the conduct of the child. Thus, as Robert Park concluded in 1935, "The community, including the family, with its wider interests, its larger purposes, and its more deliberate aims, surrounds us, includes us, and compels us to conform."

In the prevention and treatment of delinquency, it would seem desirable to use these natural human resources in the community. Because of their prestige value, natural groups and institutions are of vital social significance. Through them, local citizens can display their initiative and abilities in developing a constructive program for themselves, their children, and their neighbors. Such use of these natural leaders and groups should be of distinct therapeutic value to those who are dealing with the individual on a psychiatric or case work basis. As a product of the characteristic social life of the community, natural leaders and groups can be utilized to give constructive direction to the cultural and recreational life of the community.

These communities are already operating on a basis of leadership, but many times it is a destructive leadership. Therefore, serious consideration should be given to the possibilities of utilizing this leadership along more socially constructive lines. Little could be suggested that would improve the status of these natural leaders, but through guidance and modification of their attitudes, changes may be effected through them in the younger members of the community who respond to them.

With regard to the utilization of lay leaders in a recreation program, James S. Plant, an outstanding authority in the field of psychiatry, made the following comments in 1937:

> ... Wherever a person collects about himself a neighborhood group "for a game of old cat" recreational experiences begin to be institutionalized. These informal groups may have in them the untrammeled spontaneity of each individual's desire to play or they may be regimented by the martinet. So far as the former situation obtains it is obviously our task to do no more than catch and strengthen this type of leadership. Here, it seems to

us, lies the most sincere and serious problem in recreation development. . . .

Social service leaders recognize that recreation in itself does not offer a solution to the problem of delinquency. Provisions for recreation and cultural development are significant to the extent that they are communitywide in scope, and to the extent that they actually embody the socially desirable ideals and purposes of the community.

The effectiveness of recreation and many other welfare activities as therapeutic measures, it is assumed, could be greatly enhanced if such programs were evolved as community enterprises, integrated with the indigenous groups of the community, and so interpreted to the local residents that they became an expression of the efforts of the community itself to promote its own welfare. Thus, the program is developed *with* rather than *for* the local community. This procedure avoids differentiation between members of the professional staff and residents of the local community, and the implication of a relationship of subordination and superordination between the servers and the served.

Although the importance of local groups and local leadership is stressed in this book, it is equally important to recognize that many of the problems that confront these deteriorated local communities are citywide in scope. Crime is not a matter of personal or neighborhood blame. It is an infectious growth organically related to the whole social structure of the city. Even citizens who appear infinitely removed from its circumstance are perhaps subtly involved in its causation.

It therefore becomes a duty of the residents of the more privileged areas to join forces with the residents of these poorer areas in coping with these problems. This means not only making money and facilities available, but also recognizing (1) that the residents of the poorer communities are the most seriously concerned and personally interested and have the most at stake; (2) that their practices, attitudes, and standards are the most significant to the child in his or her response to the social world; and (3) that it is these people who are in the most strategic position to put into effect any plan for molding the character of the youth of the community.

THE SPECIFIC FEATURES OF THE CHICAGO AREA PROJECT

The Chicago Area Project, as its name implies, is an attempt to treat the problem of delinquency by means of a community-wide program based on the principles discussed in this book. Since rates of delinquency and crime are excessively high in particular areas in the city, it would seem that intensive effort is necessary to cope with the problem in these areas. If juvenile delinquency is, in large measure, characteristic of certain segments of the social life of these areas, it seems feasible to assume that one approach to a solution of the problem would be through constructive changes in the attitudes, practices, and moral standards that prevail in the neighborhood as a whole. The precise methods to be employed in bringing about these changes are not known, but, as John Dewey observed in 1922:

> To change the "working character" or will of another, we have to alter objective conditions which enter into his habits. Our own schemes of judgment, of assigning blame and praise, of awarding punishment and honor are part of these conditions. . . . We cannot change habit directly; that notion is magic. But we can change it indirectly by modifying conditions, by an intelligent selecting and weighing of the objects which engage attention and which influence the fulfillment of desires.

That the approach made by the Area Project is based on sound theory is indicated by Harry Stack Sullivan's succinct comment on the findings of the Symposium on Mental Health, held in connection with the Annual Meeting of the American Association for the Advancement of Science, Richmond, Virginia, December 28–30, 1938:

> This session of the Symposium has taught us that we must study
> people as people, in the setting of the times and in their actual
> social-cultural environment, if we are to uncover the factors that
> make for failure and mental disorder on the one hand, for success
> and mental health, on the other. There are many fields of data
> to be covered, many complex factors to be uncovered and as-
> sessed. The exploration calls for scientists who are intensely
> interested in man and his actual conduct among men and man-
> made institutions, not in parts of the human body nor yet in pale
> abstract formulae about people, or money, or work or play.

The Area Project is essentially an effort on the part of local residents, working in conjunction with the local agencies and institutions, to create a body of constructive sentiments, ideals, and practices of such scope and vitality as to influence significantly the life of every child in the community. At present, many boys and girls in certain areas grow up under the influence of groups or persons who lead them into delinquency and crime. It is hoped that by enlisting the efforts of local residents in a program to promote the cause of human welfare, constructive values may be made more universal in the community. Perhaps constructive leadership may, in time, be substituted for the destructive leadership that now influences the lives of many of the children in the neighborhood.

The Area Project is, briefly, an application of the fundamental principles that are basic to any truly democratic social order: that in the humble environs of the community itself, the good common sense, the deep concern of the parent in his or her child's future, the mutual respect of neighbor for neighbor, the motivations that everyone shares to command the respect and admiration of their fellows, and the common struggle for the simple satisfactions of life can be found the necessary strength and leadership for the solution of local community problems.

Applying these principles to the development of programs in deteriorated areas is perhaps much more feasible today than ever before. At present, the percentage of native-born residents in the population is much greater than it was two or three decades ago. This native-born population, which is thoroughly sophisticated with regard to the American life, comprises a constructive resource that was previously not available to those interested in community welfare, especially social settlements and other earlier forms of group work enterprises.

The specific features of the Area Project plan may be briefly summarized as follows.

1. Use of "Natural" Leaders.   In each area neighborhood activities have been organized and operated under the sponsorship of a community committee, composed of local residents who are important "natural leaders" in community life. For the most part, these are persons who have achieved prestige as members of significant neighborhood institutions. They are church leaders, lawyers, doctors, dentists, students, shopkeepers, druggists, undertakers and rank-and-file residents of the community. It is their function to help plan, control, and give moral support to the program. Each committee is divided into various subcommittees, which assume specific responsibilities.

2. Staff.   With the exception of a small number of trained workers, the staff is recruited from the neighborhood. (Variations in this procedure are adopted to correspond to different conditions in the communities.) Some receive a small stipend, while others are volunteers. As indicated later in this chapter, most of these workers have been employed by the State of Illinois. All program activities are under the supervision of the community committee, which functions in cooperation with trained staff representatives from the Illinois Commission on Delinquency Prevention and other private and public agencies. Staff meetings are held at frequent and regular intervals to discuss problems arising in the communities.

The members of the supervisory staff who have functioned with the Area Project have had training in sociology, in group work, in social work, psychiatry, and law and some have not had any specialized training.

3. Activities. Through the local committee, a program of varied recreational, cultural, and education activities is carried on in conjunction with agencies established in the community. These include camping, football, basketball, baseball, boxing, wrestling, swimming, ping-pong, pool, billiards, small table games, music, dramatics, movies, handicrafts, printing, newspaper work, club meetings, and various forms of adult education and civic activities.

The greatest possible use is made of these recreational, civic, and educational activities with a view to developing community morale, consensus, and concerted action. Such a series of activities, when utilized by the community for the purpose of elevating its moral and cultural condition, becomes a dynamic spiritual force contributing to a new morale. This is reflected in new enthusiasms in the community, acting as a moral force to encourage efforts toward better schools, playgrounds, parks, and development of other phases of cultural and social activities for the benefit of all the residents. Thus, the program takes on a much more inclusive and communitywide aspect than would one narrowed to the objective of dealing with the problem of delinquent children.

4. Social Action. Neighborhood or community committees concern themselves with conditions in the community and carry on specific campaigns to improve the environment and secure better facilities and opportunities for health, housing, employment, education, and law enforcement. Committees have (a) met with public officials to enlarge facilities in local schools or public parks; (b) presented plans to deal with housing by developing programs to demolish, conserve, or rehabilitate old buildings or submitted a plan for the urban renewal of an entire neighborhood; (c) conferred with local law enforcement officials to obtain better services to deal with traffic problems or crime on the streets; (d) met with executives of local industries to provide jobs, especially opening up new opportunities for minorities or ex-offenders; and, on occasion, (e) picketing or engaging in protest marches directed at different segments of the power structure.

5. Use of "Natural" Group.   The community committee seeks to make these activities available to all of the children of the neighborhood—delinquent and nondelinquent. There are few formal classes organized for children. Insofar as possible each child is enrolled along with the other members of the group to which he or she belongs, with the aim of preserving the natural relationships and controls in the group. In the case of the delinquent group, the task becomes one of introducing constructive values into the life and structure of the group. It is in this connection that utilization of the prestige of the natural leader is of greatest importance.

6. Use of All Community Resources.   In poor communities, there are institutions and organizations that have been developed and sustained by the financial support and initiative of persons and groups outside the community, as well as the usual institutions indigenous to the communtiy. To the largest extent possible these indigenous institutions are utilized along with public playgrounds, parks, and neighborhood agencies.

By proceeding on this basis, it is possible for the neighborhood committee to consider the needs of the community as a whole and to develop a communitywide program in which all existing facilities are utilized.

It seems reasonable to assume that a coordination of all facilities would yield more constructive results than would a procedure in which neighborhood institutions function more or less independently of each other.

Overhead cost in terms of buildings, equipment, and other material resources is minimized when the entire resources of the community already at the disposal of the lay people themselves—church buildings, club centers, community centers, public agencies, parks, and private homes—are utilized in this general program of community action.

7. News Bulletins.   In some areas a news bulletin is printed and circulated by the residents. This serves to propagandize the program, arouse general public interest, stimulate concerted action, and contribute to vocational and educational training.

8. Forums.   Public meetings of various kinds are promoted by the community committee in the neighborhood to provide opportunities for discussion by local residents of matters pertaining to community welfare. On such occasions, the purposes of the activities program are defined and interpreted to the community. The aim of these forums is to create a consciousness on the part of the community regarding local problems, to crystallize public opinion, and to stimulate the residents to act collectively for community betterment.

9. The Delinquent Child. Although delinquents are not set apart in the neighborhood program, particular effort is made to see that their needs are met in centers set up by the community committee or through facilities offered by other agencies in the neighborhood. A place is made for them in an organized system of activities, offering, through the added discipline of local leadership, an intensive supervision and a personal guidance not feasible under the present system of probation or parole.

In dealing with some of the delinquents, special services are secured from child guidance clinics, family case work agencies, courts, hospitals, and other organizations that offer intensive individual and case work treatment.

10. Research and Experimentation. The Chicago Area Project is experimental in the sense that it is formulated on the basis of certain assumptions regarding the nature of the problem of delinquency in deteriorated areas. As already indicated, these assumptions suggest an approach to a solution of the problem directed toward community reorganization and rehabilitation, to supplement work already offered through psychiatric and family case work services. The effectiveness of this approach is tested in various ways. This does not mean that the children in these areas are subjected to tests or observations or to any kind of activity not characteristic of established agencies. No claims for the program in any neighborhood are made until support of objective evidence is available for them.

The Area Project attempts to utilize principles already widely accepted. Its basic ideas and principles are not new—

they are as old as democratic society. Therefore, the answer to the question "Is not the Area Project primarily a research or experimental enterprise?" is that the difference from established social or civic welfare agencies that exists lies not in the ultimate goals but in the steps taken to achieve those goals.

THE CHICAGO AREA PROJECT AFTER FORTY YEARS

The Chicago Area Project, based on the principles just described, was launched in 1934, in three low-income neighborhoods in Chicago. Over the years the Project has been developed in approximately 30 other neighborhoods and in a number of downstate communities in Illinois. Since this enterprise was a forerunner of the many community-based programs developed during the past decade, a fuller account and progress report of this pioneer venture in community organization is in order.

Many years of experience have demonstrated the validity and feasibility of the principle of carrying on welfare programs in local communities on this basis. Where this program has been in operation for a number of years, experience has shown that responsible citizen groups become vital instruments in meeting the needs of children, expecially children who get into difficulties. This method of cooperative self-help applied to local community problems has been a powerful stimulus to residents. Heretofore untapped human resources of the neighborhood are mobilized for a concerted and collective attack on human problems. Citizens and local leaders know their community intimately, have personal contacts and relationships with the significant social world of the delinquent, and can, therefore, make a distinctive contribution toward the solution of local problems.

Through the instruments of independent community or neighborhood committees, local residents have pooled their knowledge and coordinated their efforts to achieve goals that no single resident could attain unaided. In such creative, cooperative efforts, the self-reliance of the individual is strengthened, his or her sense of pride and work is enhanced, and he or she discovers through experience the strength inherent in the common bonds that tie one neighbor to another. In addition, the common interests and sentiments developed among residents through their participation and leadership in constructive endeavors for the improvement of their community eventually instill incentives toward conformity to the conventional life of the community in the child.

Briefly, this program has been based on certain assumptions regarding the nature of delinquency: "(1) that the problem of delinquency in low-income areas is to a large extent the product of the social experiences to which children and young people are customarily exposed; (2) that effective treatment and prevention can be achieved only so far as constructive changes in the community life can be brought about; (3) that effective rehabilitation entails the re-incorporation of the offender into some socially constructive group or groupings in the community; and (4) that in any enterprise which is likely to be effective in bringing about these changes, it is indispensable that the local residents, individually and collectively, accept the fullest possible responsibility for defining objectives, formulating policies, finding financial support and exercising the necessary control over budgets, personnel and programs."

The principles and the strategy of the Area Project just described have as much validity today as when they were formulated over 40 years ago. Tested pragmatically in a wide variety of neighborhoods, these principles are summarized as follows.

1. The neighborhood is the unit of operation.
2. Planning and management is in the hands of local residents.
3. Local workers should be on the staff.

4. Community resources should be more fully utilized and coordinated.
5. Credit should be given to local residents.

These principles clearly contradict sharply most current practices. They become intelligible, however, only when viewed in terms of the whole history of the Area Project and Shaw's unique philosophy.

The principles and policies of the Chicago Area Project grew out of the practical experiences and studies of Clifford Shaw. But this program is related also to Shaw's deep concern for individuals involved in difficulties. Throughout his career as a probation and parole officer, and later as research sociologist at the Institute for Juvenile Research and director of the Area Project, Clifford Shaw had intimate contact with hundreds of youthful and adult offenders. He had unusual insight into their problems and an extraordinary ability in assisting them in working out satisfactory adjustments.

To Clifford Shaw, a delinquent was not a "case" but a human being endowed with human traits, capacities, and feelings. He rejected the idea that the offender is innately inadequate or defective, and he constantly focused attention on the fact that our society often creates problems for the delinquent. Shaw especially rebelled at the way society wittingly or unwittingly rejected, stigmatized, and "cast out" the delinquent from conventional groups. He reacted with indignation at the impersonal machinery that society sets up to treat the delinquent. While Clifford Shaw recognized that institutional treatment of the delinquent is at times necessary, he warned the public that such measures often tend to dehumanize both the offender and the institutional personnel. In his writings and public speeches he constantly urged that we should always keep the human needs of the young offender in focus.

Shaw often stressed the fact that the typical delinquent is detached or alienated from conventional groups. He pointed out that in inner-city areas the offender is usually a member of a gang or street-corner group that is unreached and, therefore, influenced little by the character-building agencies and other welfare institutions. Shaw, therefore, urged that better methods were needed to reach the autonomous and hostile street-corner groups and redirect them into the conventional life of the community. Shaw firmly believed that one of the most valuable resources available to any community, in attempting to deal with the problem of delinquency prevention or rehabilitation, is the residents and neighborhood leaders. He stated (1944):

> The local neighborhood can be organized to deal effectively with its own problems. The less privileged areas of a city such as Chicago contain sufficient indigenous leadership to bring about the necessary changes in attitudes, sentiments, ideals and loyalties for the construction of a more acceptable community life. In these areas are remarkable untapped resources in human leadership. The reduction of delinquency depends upon the extent to which the people themselves, however, understand and want a program of community betterment and are willing to work for it and call it their own.

Shaw realized well the importance of social movements and reforms that would in time, perhaps, improve conditions in the disadvantaged communities. But he regarded these efforts as segmental and long range, leaving untouched the immediate basic community conditions. For this reason, he worked fervently and assiduously for over 25 years to develop the Area Project, which he firmly believed was formulated on principles that were logically sound and consistent with democratic practice and humanitarian values.

Clifford Shaw's death in August 1957, was an irreplaceable loss. However, he left a legacy of ideas and practices that still inspire his associates and the thousands of residents and workers in local communities throughout the nation. The Chicago Area Project, therefore, continues as a truly fitting living memorial to an outstanding social scientist, a humanitarian in the truest sense of that term, and a great leader of a significant social movement.

Clifford Shaw's studies and the Chicago Area Project have undoubtedly had a constructive impact on welfare work generally. Witness, for example, the many new community and neighborhood programs that have been launched in recent years with the slogans, "reaching the unreached," "hard to reach youth projects," and similar programs that stress utilizing the constructive resources of the community. Speaking on the subject, "Delinquents: Outcasts of Society," Bertram Beck (1954) said:

> I find it rather odd to be speaking on this topic in Chicago, for it was in this City some 30 years ago that Clifford Shaw and his associates embarked on their series of studies that dramatically illustrated the manner in which we failed to reach delinquent children and their families, and served as the basis of one of the most significant experiments in reaching the unreached that continues to this day. Clifford Shaw's early works were not well received by the social work profession. Perhaps, it was that we, as a young profession, were overly sensitive to criticism and he, as a stalwart enthusiast, was less than delicate. Or perhaps it was that he, like all men of rare ability, was ahead of his times.[2]

As already mentioned, the principles and methods underlying the work of the Area Project grew out of the studies and research projects carried on since 1926, by Shaw, McKay, and other collaborators on the staff of the Sociological Services of the Institute for Juvenile Research, a division of the Illinois Department of Public Welfare. The Chicago Area Project, as a private corporation with a board of directors of prominent citizens interested in welfare work, was organized in 1934. The Board of Directors is responsible for raising and disbursing the private funds required to carry on studies and research, and for

[2]Remarks by Bertram M. Beck, Director, Special Juvenile Delinquency Project, U.S. Children's Bureau at a meeting of the Welfare Council of Metropolitan Chicago, April 5, 1954.

providing occasional financial assistance to individual community committees, usually on a matching basis.

Until June 30, 1957, the field services personnel or community organizers and consultants to local citizens were on the staff of the Sociological Services of the Institute for Juvenile Research. On July 1, of the same year, by act of the Legislature, most of this staff, approximately 35 persons, were transferred to the Illinois Youth Commission, an administrative agency established in 1954, to coordinate and integrate all of the state's services for the treatment of delinquents and the prevention of delinquency. The persons transferred constituted the Division of Community Services of the Youth Commission until 1968. In 1969, this agency was transferred into the new Department of Corrections, Juvenile Division. On January 1, 1976, this staff was transferred into the Illinois Commission on Delinquency Prevention.

Thirty separate neighborhood committees have developed in Chicago. These independent, self-governing citizen groups, operating under their own names and charters, are the core of this program of community action. The areas in which local committees operate vary in size from approximately ½ square mile to 2½ square miles with a population ranging from 10,000 to 50,000. These citizen committees, the Board of Directors of the Chicago Area Project, and the agencies of the State that furnish personnel represent the Chicago Area Project.[3]

The resources usually needed to launch and establish self-directed organizations of residents in the different areas of the city are as follows: (1) trained personnel made available by the State of Illinois, (2) initial financial assistance by the Board of Directors of the Chicago Area Project on a matching basis to local community committees, and (3) assistance to local committees in their search for other sources of funds. For example,

[3]Similar community programs in downstate Illinois are described by Muriel Martin, "People Who Care," *Illinois Education Association.* Vol. 24, No. 9, May, 1962.

today sixteen community committees receive a part of their budget from the Community Fund of Chicago.

The role of state personnel is to help the independent citizen groups to attain their objectives. To this end, staff members function either as consultants or community workers in relation to the activities of the local committee. As the committees approach the point of self-sufficiency, they are encouraged to dispense with the services of state-employed personnel in favor of their own paid personnel. In some instances, this goal has already been achieved. Thereafter state personnel are available only as consultants.

The staff organization of neighborhood committees typically includes one or more state employees who function either as consultants or program directors. In addition, each committee also employs its own program specialists, either part or full time.

Each community organization identified with the Area Project is an independent, autonomous unit chartered as a nonprofit corporation, with its own headquarters and office. Some committees have developed subcenters or branches. While programs and the organizational structure of specific groups may vary to some degree, each community committee conducts programs designed to (1) provide special facilities for work with groups of delinquent children at the neighborhood level, (2) bring local neighborhood leaders into youth and community welfare programs, both in the formulation and execution of policy, (3) aid area residents in developing a better understanding of the problems of children and youth through special adult education projects, (4) assist local institutions and public officials to enlarge and make the services that they render to the community more effective, (5) improve recreational, educational, and other community services to children, and (6) foster the physical and social improvement of the neighborhood through a variety of methods.

The neighborhood committees identified with the Area Project have engaged in a variety of activities. They have (1) promoted programs of recreation and sports involving thousands of children and young people and, in two instances, purchased and built their own summer camps, (2) secured access to churches and other significant local institutions and groups usually not available for neighborhood welfare programs, (3) improved relationships between the schools and communities by helping in several instances to organize parent–teacher associations and other groups for adult education, and (4) led campaigns for community improvement and in several instances initiated the formation of housing boards.

An especially encouraging aspect of the work of the neighborhood committees has been in the treatment of delinquents and older offenders. In an effort to help as many delinquents as possible, the citizen groups have organized working arrangements with the Youth Bureau of the Chicago Police Department, the Cook County Juvenile Court, and with other probation and parole systems. In instances where the initial work in the neighborhood fails, local residents seek to maintain contact with the delinquent when he or she is in court; in the institution, if he or she is committed; and, of course, again in the community when the delinquent returns on parole. This work with young people on parole from correctional institutions has been one of the most promising aspects of this program. In four or five neighborhoods where intensive work has been carried on, local residents have had unusual success in reincorporating offenders in conventional groups. In many instances the offenders become members of the local community committee, often serve on Boards of Directors, and are sometimes elected as officers of the committee.

In dealing with juvenile delinquents, the work with individuals has been supplemented by efforts to deal with the gang as a whole through the use of local leaders. As a matter of fact, when a program is launched in a neighborhood, the local worker often has already begun by contacting local gangs and street-corner groups. This procedure has enabled the workers and citizens' groups to obtain basic information that is necessary for the planning and development of the program. At the same time, it has served as a beginning for a systematic effort by the community to establish communication and liaison with the world of the delinquent. For 40 years work with boys' and girls' groups and street-corner groups has been an integral part of the programs of some of the community committees. Local leaders have little or no difficulty in reaching street-corner groups. Young adult workers, who symbolize values that are meaningful to the youngsters, are thus in a strategic position to guide the groups into constructive activities.

The work carried on by neighborhood committees is discussed later in this volume, together with the difficulties and problems encountered in such community programs. Similarly, some of the problems in evaluating the effectiveness of these programs are also discussed. However, the Area Project approach is based on the logic that the delinquents and their groups must first be reached before they can be helped. Most of the delinquent groups, especially the habitual and severely delinquent groups, are often outside the sphere of influence of conventional social agencies and often do not regard themselves as problems and hence do not seek treatment. This suggests that a meaningful approach to the problem of group delinquency requires attempts to control and redirect the activities of delinquent groups.

The community programs of the Chicago Area Project pointed the way by which delinquents could be reached more effectively and suggested efforts that could be made to "change the street" through the organized efforts of local residents. While all types of services, facilities, and programs are necessary to deal more effectively with the overall problem of delinquency in our cities, our limited success to reduce the volume of delinquency through traditional efforts suggests that we still need to discover more effective methods. What we must ultimately do to prevent delinquency is to stabilize and integrate the local community and change the moral world of the child.

This point was best made many years ago by the late Dr. Plant (1937), who said:

> Society is, and has been, aroused over its misfits and the mass of human breakdown that is in the wake of its progress. It has erected every conceivable type of agency to study, salvage or merely sweep up this debris. As the wreckage mounts, new agencies are demanded or "better standards" asked of those existing. The folly of believing that happiness and goodness can be fabricated by machinery (agencies) will be exposed only when we understand that the ills, corruptions and hypocrisies of a cultural pattern flow into the child and man and "become a part of him for the day, for the year or for stretching cycles of years."
>
> If it is true that the triumphs and tragedies of the street flow into and become a part of the child, then all programs of personality change must manage somehow to change the street.[4]

While no blueprint is available that would achieve Dr. Plant's goal to "change the street," no one would deny the importance, indeed the indispensability, of involving local residents on a neighborhood basis as participants in any enterprise to deal with community problems. More and more it is being recognized that a basic requirement in any program designed to help people with problems is to devise better methods of bringing the affected populations as participants in the enterprise. Unless this is done we are not likely to succeed in fostering new values, new goals, and new action patterns essential to the development of any community enterprise.

Without question the community programs suggested by the Chicago Area Project can bring a new kind of resource into the battle for delinquency prevention—a resource that is available, ready to be tapped in every community, even the most disorderly and disorganized ones. Even where the problem is most acute, there is to be found talent, leadership, power, and

[4]The late Dr. Plant was for years a psychiatrist in charge of the Essex County Juvenile Court.

interest in participation. Case histories of neighborhoods that have demonstrated the feasibility and validity of this basic idea are presented later in this volume.

SUMMARY

The findings of the sociological studies of delinquency by Shaw, McKay, and others have generally suggested that the roots of delinquency and crime were to be found in the conditions of life prevailing in the low-income areas of the city. Studies of boys' and girls' own stories have indicated that delinquent careers usually have a long history and that there is little prospect of solution through easy or quick solutions. Traditional methods of prevention and treatment have had limited success.

The implications of the above findings generally indicate that community conditions must be modified in any effective program of treatment and prevention, that a better way must be found to reach the delinquents and their groups and redirect them into the conventional life of the community, that new facilities and resources for children are needed, that improvements in general living conditions must take place, and finally that in any such efforts local residents individually and collectively need to be actively involved in planning and carrying on the program.

In keeping with this conception of the nature of the problems this writer is of the strong conviction, based on 40 years of experience, that the greatest resource available is the human resource, the residents of neighborhoods and local areas. As Clifford Shaw always stressed: "We need to build within the neighborhood of the delinquent a human instrument—organizations of citizens. Wherever you have a group of people thinking and working together you are developing a constructive element—introducing a certain stability, developing common purposes. These human resources—talents and leadership of local residents—are close to and significant to the child. They constitute a force which is natural, available and valuable."

Chapter 3

BUILDING A NEIGHBORHOOD
ORGANIZATION

PART ONE

ORGANIZATIONAL ISSUES

Nothing offers a greater chance for combating delinquency than a mobilized neighborhood once it is jolted out of its apathy, and once it begins positive, cooperative action. The trouble is, how do you mobilize it? How do you get people to work together?

I have seen neighborhood and community efforts fail and succeed. The most common cause of failure comes from not recruiting leadership from the grassroots—the indigenous leaders, the residents themselves. Sometimes community efforts fail because one person attempts to dominate and hence volunteers shy away from that heavy hand. When organizations are taken over by professionals or politically motivated leaders, the lay leaders tend to become suspicious and they ease out of the organization for fear of being used. As one such person said, "I don't want to be done good on by no do-gooder." When the people living in an area who are to be the recipients of the services are not brought into the planning, it results in one-sided giving. No one wants to be on the receiving end all the time. A community organizer, whether a professional staff person or lay leader, must avoid some of these pitfalls if a viable neighborhood organization is to be developed.

During recent decades, deterioration of physical environment and disruption of social institutions in city neighborhoods and particularly inner city neighborhoods has greatly increased. There is growing anger and alienation among residents of urban neighborhoods. A sense of powerlessness and frustration prevails among many residents of these areas because of their inability to influence the attitudes and behavior of the leaders of the power structure with regard to the allocation of resources and other public policy decisions that profoundly affect their immediate environments and, therefore, their lives.

In keeping with democratic ideals of personal freedom, equality of opportunity, and humane living conditions, every effort should be made to deal with problems of city neighborhoods in terms of participatory democracy. We should no longer, as so often happened in the past, impose programs or policies on local residents but involve them in enterprises for social action to improve the neighborhood and the wider community.

As indicated in the previous chapter, small groups of citizens have organized on a neighborhood basis thereby attesting to the strength of the belief in self-determination and self-improvement. In recent years, federal policy has encouraged, and to some extent institutionalized, "maximum feasible participation" and "effective representation in decisions that affect the local community."

Some of the procedures, guidelines, and strategies for mobilizing the talents and leadership of local residents to deal with youth problems, delinquency and related social problems are discussed as follows.

To organize a citizens' group of any kind is not easy. It is especially difficult to do so when one's primary goal is not easily measured in immediate results—and this is certainly true of an aim as the prevention of delinquency.

Some of the problems one must face include recruiting volunteers (who are the prime ingredient) with the time, interest, and willingness to join, but are few and far between. The organizer faces great odds. Any known good volunteers may already be committed to other programs; the population of the area may have recently changed so that good volunteers are unknown; most residents may be apathetic, afraid, in despair, "fed-up with do-gooders," disillusioned by having been misled or misused by previous organizers; or so busy "making ends meet" that they do not have time for a committee. People may have many reasons for not wanting to join a neighborhood organization. Organizers face a tremendous challenge when they begin their task. But if they have faith in people, a conviction in the principles of self-help, patience, boundless energy, tact, and perseverance, they can succeed.

The organization of self-help neighborhood committees in disadvantaged areas is a relatively new development in efforts to cope with social problems. The assumption that committees can be organized for delinquency prevention in any neighborhood of any urban or rural area is sound. As indicated in the previous chapter, the Chicago Area Project has, since 1934, been assisting neighborhoods in some of the areas of high delinquency in Chicago. The question is not can it be done, but how is it done?

Beyond a few basic ideas, not too much advice can be offered for creating a new neighborhood committee. One criterion or measurement of success, however, is obvious. If a truly successful volunteer program is developed, then the organizer should be able to minimize his or her role and ultimately to withdraw completely in a reasonable time. However, as a committee develops an ongoing, active program, some staff will always be needed. Because areas vary in many respects and because there are countless forces at play that make each area distinct, the truths discovered by one worker or the success achieved by another may mislead a new worker. What has worked in one area may not in another. What failed in one area may be most effective in another. The suggestions are offered for the purpose of providing possible ideas, not probable guarantees of success.

Most answers sought by community workers will come about through daily growth in their understanding and from their experiences in the area in which they are serving. After a time, they may realize that answers to the basic issues and the problems in their area must come from the residents. Seldom does the expert downtown have the insight or knowledge necessary for the solutions to an area's problems. As the saying goes, it should be "an inside job."

THE COMMUNITY WORKER

Throughout this book the organizer is referred to as a community worker, which is the job classification used by state employees in Illinois engaged in promoting the Chicago Area Project, local youth commissions, and other types of citizens' groups. This arrangement between a state agency—the Commission on Delinquency Prevention—and private corporations is unique. However, other states, municipalities, or even private agencies who might wish to sponsor neighborhood organizations of the type discussed in this book could utilize other public or private sources to employ community workers for such an undertaking.

The role of the community worker with the Chicago program is to help the independent citizen groups to attain their objectives. To this end, staff members function either as consultants or community workers in relation to the activities of the local committee. The staff organization usually consists of a district supervisor who has the responsibility for community workers assigned to a geographic area. A community worker usually covers a relatively small neighborhood or natural area and assists the committee in achieving its objectives. However, some committees also employ their own program specialists, either part or full time.

Community work calls for skill in the organizer in identifying the residents holding key positions of influence and the ability to arouse interest in youth welfare activities. The professional worker must have knowledge of the local society and a capacity for sympathetic identification with the local residents. Thus, the worker should be familiar with the culture of the local society, its history, background of ethnic groups, and local institutions, and with the power structure through which decisions are made and executed, and with the conflicts and cleavages that orient and align the population.

From the inception of this program, it became evident that qualified local workers offered advantages in the establishment of such programs. In the first place, the indigenous worker usually possesses a natural knowledge of the community. Second, he or she is usually not hampered by barriers to communication with residents. Third, he or she is more likely than the nonresident to have access to the neighborhood's delinquents and, therefore, likely to be more effective in redirecting their conduct.

The first essential qualification in community workers is their ability to maintain effective relationships with all segments of the community and particularly with the indigenous leadership. The workers need to be thoroughly conventional with regard to their own attitudes, values, and goals so that they will not engage in marginal or unconventional conduct. Community workers must be tolerant and understanding of those who do not share their values and life goals, such as the delinquent, the criminal, the addict, and other nonconformists. However, this does not mean that the workers cannot disapprove of the activities of these persons, but rather that they not reject these persons as outcasts because of their delinquent activities.

A second criterion is that the workers must be especially secure in their own social group. In working with groups, the workers must be content with a special role outside the status arrangements of the members of the group, and not place themselves in a competitive position with the members of the group in order to meet their own needs. In our type of program, where the emphasis is on building up local leadership, the workers must not maneuver themselves into the role of the indispensable leader.

Since it has not been established what type of training or education is necessary for effective work with delinquents, we operate in keeping with the point of view expressed above. We endeavor first to select a person with the desired personality characteristics suggested above and we are quite flexible with regard to formal education. In most instances, however, our community workers are high school graduates, and many have several years of college. Most of our supervisors are college graduates with majors in sociology. We encourage workers to continue their education, we provide tuition for special courses, and, of course, we carry on in-service training.

SURVEY OF THE NEIGHBORHOOD

While the nature and scope of neighborhood problems may be evident from statistical data of the courts and schools and from other sources, a comprehensive survey is also necessary to determine the concentration, involvement, environmental structure, economic stability, and other characteristics of the community.

The community worker through assistance from community volunteers should survey the nature of youth problems in the area by interviewing logical sources of information such as law enforcement agencies, school officials, judges, ministers, merchants, caseworkers, teenage and civic leaders, staff members of recreational agencies, and others. During the interviews, records should be maintained of the data that will be helpful in structuring the program to meet the problem. Preparing a card index file of the names of apparent leaders and potential members of the community committees will be of particular importance to the community worker.

When talking to local people, it is important that community workers identify themselves and their assignment. They should explain their role and indicate which institution or organization is employing them and sponsoring the program.

RECRUITING VOLUNTEERS

After the survey is completed, then the second phase of the community worker's responsibility is to share the findings with a few local leaders. Then comes the recruitment of people to help form a neighborhood organization.

A period of several months may be needed to recruit a nucleus for the first meeting. During the preliminary contacts, the community worker should ask those who show interest when they would care to schedule a meeting, and where they would like to meet.

Care should be given in selecting the site for the first meeting. The size of the attendance will be a factor. The place selected should be comfortable, quiet, and conveniently located. The best source for a meeting place would be one of the rooms designated for this purpose usually found in schools, civic buildings, and fraternal organizations. Some programs have started in the homes of local residents. Many people are more comfortable for a first meeting in the kitchen or living room of a neighborhood.

When planning the first meeting, the worker should ask those interested to suggest subjects that might be discussed. The worker should also prepare a statement to be made at the first meeting specifying what services and other resources the worker may be expected to provide, such as mimeographing, pictures, maps or charts, and films or slides. At this time the community worker should explain that he or she can function with the group on condition that the membership is open to all residents of the area and that the committee remains non-denominational and nonpolitical. The venture is a partnership between many segments of the community to help in the prevention of delinquency. Some funds may be needed almost from the beginning and the worker should encourage the nucleus of volunteers to explore sources. Some funds may be available from local sources, if the need is shown and the local group has expressed an interest in doing what it can with its own resources.

Once a nucleus of five or more agree, the meeting can be held. It should be informal. Such questions as the name, area, and objectives can be discussed, but the importance of avoiding hasty decisions should be stressed. An attendance sheet with the names, addresses, and phone numbers can prove useful. It may be necessary at the first meeting for the community worker to explain the work again so that everyone involved understands his or her role.

An accurate record, not only of those in attendance but also of the subjects discussed and any decisions reached, should be made for two reasons. First, it establishes a proper precedent of businesslike procedure, and, second, it enables persons who affiliate subsequent to this meeting to be privy to previous action.

The following considerations are recommended to enlist the largest number of volunteers:

General Promotion and Volunteer Recruitment

The first part of the campaign, the *general promotion,* will utilize "soft-sell" techniques. Its purpose will be to develop knowledge of and good will toward the program in the community. It should develop interest, concern, and awareness of the problems. Such a campaign should be divided in three parts:

1. *Publicity.* There will be a strong reluctance on the part of the people in the community to participate as members of the committee unless they are conditioned about its scope, needs, and general acceptance. It is imperative that the entire program be publicized through an intense campaign conducted through the local community press, institutional bulletins, and other media.
2. *Recruitment.* The entire intent of the delinquency prevention program is to solicit the assistance of the members of the community, organize them into functioning groups, and eventually make them self-sustaining so that the community worker may proceed to other areas that need attention. Through an emotional, as well as rational appeal, the community worker will look for people regardless of their educational or economic backgrounds by going into homes and stores and by attending meetings of local organizations, informal groups, clubs, societies, and the like.

The community worker should anticipate such questions as: "Why are you asking me?" and "What can I do?" In response, he or she should explain the value of neighbors working together: that they can help children stay out of trouble and that a committee is a powerful means of getting better services and correcting bad situations.

The worker should point out that the residents can build *their* committee for *their* neighborhood. The ideas, the planning, the decisions, the programs, and the achievements will be *theirs.* The worker should build *the residents'* egos and confidence in themselves and avoid involving an entire existing group as the main force for the new committee. It would be better for the worker to recruit individual members from ongoing groups so that no clique can dominate the new committee.

The community worker should be aware that minority groups have now reached a point where they are aggressively active in demanding to be the *major part* of determining the destiny of their group—and that the superimposed or preconceived ideas of others are less than acceptable.

Three general sources of volunteers are:

(a) The residents of the neighborhood. This group constitutes the largest potential source. The door-to-door approach has many possibilities that demand time and persistent effort. Every area has people who can be, and want to be, invited to improve the life of the community, especially for the youth.

(b) Another source is the ongoing organized groups in churches, clubs, PTA's and fraternal and service groups such as social-athletic clubs, veterans lodges, and other groups.

(c) Outside sources include the Volunteer Bureau of Welfare Councils, citywide and statewide organizations, unions, teachers, and culture and hobby groups.

3. *The Recruitment Process.* The recruiter, whether a staff member or volunteer, should be identified as a bona fide member of the committee. If the recruiter is a staff member, he or she should, if necessary, produce written identification. The volunteer should be able to show a membership card or other evidence of authentic identity. These precautions are useful to reassure strangers of the legitimacy of the recruiter's visit. During the recruiting process, as well as all other contacts, the recruiter should:

(a) *Make a good impression* by presenting himself or herself in a manner that is most pleasing. The recruiter should be sincere, enthusiastic, and reflect convictions about the importance of the appeal he or she is making for volunteers.

(b) The recruiter should be a *pleasant conversationalist* and be willing to spend time building friendly relationships. To persuade a person to volunteer his or her services may require several contacts. The community worker should try to sell the need for help.

FORMAL ORGANIZATION

The organizational structure suggested here is a "neighborhood or community committee." However, even in the Chicago Area Project some citizens refer to their neighborhood organizations as a "youth service committee," "big buddies," "youth boosters," and so on. Citizens in different communities will choose to select the name they believe is most appropriate for their cause. The important point, however, is that all the groups are self-governing, autonomous, and chartered as nonprofit corporations, many with state and federal tax-exempt status.

In this early phase of establishing the group, some fun and social activity can do wonders to develop cohesion and raise morale of the persons present. Alternating business meetings with leisure-time fun sessions should be considered and discussed with the leaders.

If the first meeting results in a decision to organize fully, the worker should promote thinking on procedure for the selection of officers such as a chairman, vice-chairman, a treasurer, and a secretary. Generally at the first meeting a temporary chairman is selected to preside and a temporary secretary is appointed to take notes or minutes of what takes place.

The worker should give careful thought to these "temporary" assignments because they often result in the holder's being made the first permanent chairman, and so forth, and the organization then has to live with the officer for at least a year. The question of raising funds, printing stationery, establishing headquarters, and having a telephone should be faced by the leaders as these needs arise.

Simultaneously the worker should encourage key members to visit other community projects as a learning experience. Perhaps successful leaders from other neighborhood organizations could be invited to meet with the new group. In the course of a few months, short, medium, and long-range goals can be discussed at the meetings and formally adopted.

The question of incorporating as a nonprofit corporation should not be seriously faced until the group becomes stable, well-defined, and has achieved concrete success that has brought pride and confidence to the group. Bylaws can be adopted and articles of incorporation can be filed with the Secretary of State. A suggested bylaws model is found in Appendix 1. While bylaws are important, literally hundreds of previous groups have gone over the same ground exhaustively. Do not spend a disproportionate amount of the early organizational effort and time in setting up bylaws.

To increase membership and to enlighten as many local residents as possible, printed membership application forms and brochures that list the committee's objectives, program, officers, and other facts should be distributed throughout the area.

To organize a successful neighborhood committee requires not only diligent efforts but also enthusiastic attitudes and wholesome traits of character on the part of the worker. Perhaps a few "do's" and "don'ts" may be helpful for those about to organize a community group.

DO'S: Be confident, relaxed, optimistic, and sincere. Use language that is simple and clear. Give feelings of importance to the other person. Avoid such controversial topics as religion and politics. Make no promises you cannot keep.

DON'TS: Don't know it all, become impatient, press, argue, become worried or harrassed, lose your sense of humor, interrupt, keep the center of the stage, be unhappy when criticized, be noble, or become a partisan for reform.

Make the Volunteer Feel Important

Immediately after the applicant enlists as a volunteer, he or she should receive some sort of identification. To encourage enthusiasm, the paid staff should be instructed to praise the new volunteer worker for his or her interest in the welfare of others. The new volunteer should also be praised in front of the people he or she will be helping.

When the time seems appropriate, some awards should be given to the outstanding volunteer workers. These awards, based on available funds, could consist of certificates or lapel service pins. Also, recognition should be given to all of the volunteer workers for their altruistic task. One way would be to use the news media in order to publicize any of the activities carried out by any of the workers or residents. This will enhance the motivation of the volunteer worker, as Mark S. Mathews writes in *Guide to Community Actions* (Harper and Brothers, 1954).

> It is true that the major satisfaction to the individual comes from his personal feeling of a job well done, but in addition it is important to let the other people know what has been accomplished. Thoughtful programs of recognition sustain and inspire the volunteer to carry on.

PART TWO

ESTABLISHING RAPPORT WITH LOCAL INSTITUTIONS

In the rest of this chapter we discuss guidelines to facilitate building a bridge between the neighborhood committee and all the other resources in a neighborhood: the power structure, schools, agencies, and, of course, most important of all, the families and youth of the area. The community worker must never forget that his or hers is not a passive role. He or she should be available to make suggestions to the core leaders as to who to contact and how to initiate and encourage dialogue between these parties. This will enable the development of a better understanding so that a stronger and more worthwhile community spirit will come into existence.

Rapport is a necessary ingredient to establish a harmonious relationship and accord with individuals and neighborhood groups. It is necessary that there be mutual responsiveness so that every member of the group reacts spontaneously and with sympathetic understanding to the thoughts and sentiments of the others.

Rapport emanates from a deep-seated empathy and understanding of human beings and their needs in relation to their environment. It is built on respect, trust, and understanding.

Empathy is the projection of one's personality into the personality of another in order to understand him or her better.

The success of a community worker and the volunteers will depend largely on the relationship and harmony that they develop with the people whose help is needed. There will be a need to establish rapport between the resource people who will be incorporated into the effort and the various community agencies, schools, churches, private and public service groups, law enforcement agencies, and the courts.

The community worker with the committee is a key link in the numerous communication systems that make up their verbal environment. Communication is defined as a process through which relationships develop or decline and lead to growth or frustration.

Initially it will be necessary for the community worker and the volunteers to do the following:

1. Gain the interest and attention of their listeners, whether they are adults, mixed groups, or children.
2. Arouse the emotional and psychological needs of their listeners and clearly suggest to them ways whereby they may satisfy these needs.
3. Develop their goals in an understandable context and put these goals down in measurable units so that analysis of success and/or failure can be made and progress indicated on a timetable or schedule.

Achieving these goals will not be easy. The extent that the community worker and the committee achieve set goals will be a measure of their effectiveness.

THE NEIGHBORHOOD AND THE POWER STRUCTURE

It is vitally important that initial steps be taken to establish rapport with the power structure, indigenous leaders, and resource agencies. Since the prime task of the community worker is to stimulate, guide, and develop group action among the residents of a specific area, it is vital that the goodwill and cooperation of the power structure is obtained. Without a prior understanding, there may be resentment and a feeling of encroachment of the official responsibilities of the governing body. Some members of the power structure may feel that this reflects on their administration and great tact must be used to show the purpose of the worker's endeavors.

After the neighborhood committee has been organized, many other local adults should be enlisted to support the program. The neighborhood people must be convinced that the community worker and the committee are sincerely interested in helping children, and especially the problem child, make an adjustment. A sincere effort in contacting neighborhood residents of all backgrounds will result in acquiring a number of volunteers who will be willing to give assistance to those children with problems. Experience in Chicago and many downstate neighborhoods in Illinois has demonstrated that local residents from all walks of life can be enlisted. Local storekeepers, blue collar workers, skilled workers, and professional persons can all contribute in helping to carry on the youth welfare programs and community-action phases of the neighborhood committee. Indeed, if a neighborhood committee is not broadly representative of all segments of the area, it is not likely to have a viable program or meet with success in achieving its goals. Once a group of neighborhood people take an interest in these children the community worker and the committee are well on the way to success. If the schools, churches, law enforcement agencies, and the courts are aware that these children have the backing of the neighborhood committee and the worker, they will usually listen to various plans for helping the youngsters.

Again, it is important to explain the problem *fully* to all rank-and-file citizens so that the community worker and the volunteer will gain their confidence and understanding and inspire and stimulate them to contribute their time, talents, and perhaps money for the neighborhood program.

WORKING WITH LOCAL INSTITUTIONS

The community worker will find that many factors entering into the delinquent behavior pattern arise from truancy. He or she will need to have the best possible working relationships with all school personnel, particularly administrators and faculty. This can best be accomplished by having members of the neighborhood committee make contacts with the school personnel. Many times, these neighborhood sponsors or backers may be a part of the school system. Often, they may be members of the local school board. As school personnel become aware that various school board members are interested in certain problem children, closer cooperation will develop. By establishing this rapport with school personnel, the community worker will have a better chance to encourage dropouts to return to their studies.

The primary consideration in the establishment of efficient rapport between the school and the community committee lies in the worker's direction, dedication, and persistence. This source of information and contact is one of significant value inasmuch as almost all school systems today maintain permanent files of all students indicating the growth and development within the school situation. Unless this source of information can be utilized by the worker and the neighborhood committee, they will be greatly limited in the in-depth knowledge of the entire situation surrounding the particular boy or girl.

In the school systems today, there is a tremendous emphasis in the areas of guidance and counseling. Many schools require that their guidance and counseling staff take an active part in community interaction. These are the people who are dealing directly with the children day in and day out in the school situation. They are generally chosen for their ability to detect changes in behavior, to observe maturation and its related problems, and to take disciplinary measures to deter abnormal situations. It is strongly suggested, therefore, that the worker and/or members of the committee confer with the guidance department of the local school to establish contact and express an interest in working for all the children within the community. It will enable the volunteer and community worker to have a more meaningful observation of the particular child with whom they are working, and at the same time they will gain insight into behavior patterns thoroughly established prior to their contact with youth.

Most school administrators believe that they have a duty to protect as well as educate their students. At first, many administrators may be apprehensive regarding the presence and participation of the community worker and committee members within the confines of the school building. The community worker should visit school personnel regularly and not only when trouble occurs. As the administrators and guidance departments begin to relate and feel more comfortable with the community worker and the committee, the communication between them will be greatly enhanced.

It is sufficient to say that often rapport cannot be established in one, two, or even five visits. It may take a period of years before access to these areas is made completely available to the community worker. As in other businesses, one must sell himself or herself to the school personnel. After rapport is established, it will be found that the straight line of one-to-one interpersonal relationships will mushroom, and background information and records will be made available to the worker.

To establish a workable relationship with the churches and synagogues within your neighborhood, it is best to approach the problem from two directions.

1. The community worker should visit the clergy, preferably outside of the domain of the church or synagogue to ensure a more relaxed and receptive atmosphere. The cleric will probably be very interested in the goals, since he or she will have an interest in the overall well-being of the youth in the church or synagogue. To appear before the cleric only when a boy or girl is in

trouble or in need of rehabilitation obviously limits the effective working relationship. It is suggested that the community worker meet with the cleric as frequently as possible. The goals of the neighborhood committee must be explained and shown how it can be utilized and reinforced by the church or synagogue.

2. Members of the neighborhood committee and the worker should contact the people who are working actively with the youth of the church or synagogue. They should explain their interest and make themselves available for talks or assistance or as a source of information, and generally impress upon the community that they are willing to help in whatever way they can.

It is important that the community worker and the neighborhood committee maintain religious impartiality in order to deal effectively with all faiths and denominations. In these meetings, care should be taken not to challenge religious beliefs or the teachings of any church or synagogue. Any hostility in this area, real or imaginary, will greatly impair the effectiveness of the working relationship.

It must be further noted that a complete identity with the church or synagogue will also limit the numbers and the types of youth who will be willing to approach the community worker. If the worker becomes known as an arm of the church or synagogue, many of the boys and girls he or she wishes to contact may develop animosity or fear of this relationship.

It is necessary that the community worker establish rapport with law enforcement people in the various neighborhoods in which he or she works. The worker should concentrate efforts in working very closely with the juvenile officers or police who are working mainly with children with problems. The neighborhood people should be incorporated into this plan. Having a good working relationship between the neighborhood groups and the police is a *must.*

Very early in his or her assignment to an area, the community worker should also call on the judges, magistrates, court social service staff including probation officers, and the state's attorney, who represents the state at all hearings, to inform them of his or her position and role as a community worker, and express the desire to be of service in helping the young people in the community within the framework of his or her responsibilities.

The outstanding single item as far as developing rapport in working with the courts is the fact that the community worker must be around. It is recognized that the ideal situation would be for a volunteer to be available. However, this may not be possible at all times. When necessary, particularly in the early organizational stages, the community worker must make frequent visits until the volunteers can take over. The judge, magistrate, or even those involved in arraignment of the youngsters must know where to contact the volunteer or community worker. They must be able to say, "We expect the worker to be in tomorrow, or in the very near future. If not, we can call or make a personal contact with him or her." To oversimplify, it could be said that if volunteers or community workers are on hand often enough and concerned often enough and their desire to help and sincerity are made known, the court will be more than happy to use their services. It has been found that the court will use whatever tool is available to deal with the problem in a just and expedient manner. If, on the other hand, they cannot contact the volunteer or worker when they need him or her, they may be inclined not to call on their services again.

Once a favorable relationship has been established, it is quite easily maintained. The court staff will do everything within their power to utilize the services of the committee making their job easier as well as their own. Conflicts, insincerity, lack of direction, or not being readily available will create a bad image for the worker and often will lead to a poor working relationship. Experiences with the court will fail to be as rewarding to the community committee or to the people they are trying to help.

This aspect of the job of the community worker is obviously important in trying to direct delinquents from correctional institutions. The worker is, essentially, making services available as another choice in the disposition of the case. Often there appears only one choice for the youth—if the court will take advantage of the neighborhood committee's services, and if this working relationship is such that the court feels confidence in them, then it follows that the number of antagonistic commitments between youth and court will be greatly decreased.

Neighborhood committees or workers should first arrange to have a conference with the presiding judge of the juvenile court and the chief probation officer of the court, informing them of their interest in the problem of juvenile delinquency and of their willingness to help find an adult sponsor for any boy or girl whom the court might find to be in need, or the community worker's willingness to act as an adult sponsor when absolutely necessary. If the neighborhood committee has knowledge of any boy or girl who is to come before the court and thinks that they can help rehabilitate the juvenile, a committee representative should either appear at the hearing or furnish such information to the probation officer to whom the case is assigned.

In addition to the direct relationship with the court in dealing with individual cases, there should also be a general relationship with the court in the development of programs for the reduction and prevention of delinquency and the treatment of delinquents. The community worker may know of specific areas where a program is needed and should have a close enough contact with the court to enlist its support in developing such a program through the use of a neighborhood committee.

The community worker and the members of the neighborhood committee should attempt to establish relationships with colleges and universities that are located near the area of operation. Administrators and faculty members of these institutions often desire to cooperate with community organizations in an effort to give community service.

Initial contact can be made through the dean of the school or college in the university and ultimately the chairpeople of various departments—sociology, psychology, education, political science, and so on. One example of how relationships can be established is the excellent rapport between the Commission on Delinquency Prevention (before January 1, 1976, this agency was known as the Community Services Unit in the Department of Corrections) and DePaul University, through its College of Liberal Arts, particularly the Department of Sociology, the School of Education, and the School of Law.

A conference was held between the chairman of the Department of Sociology in the College of Liberal Arts and the delinquency prevention supervisor of the Community Services Unit of the Commission to determine what role DePaul University would play to become involved in the community in a more significant way in dealing with community problems and social issues of the day. As a result of this conference, a series of workshops in youth welfare, recreation, meeting planning, and the like, for community leaders and other interested persons was developed. Faculty members from various departments in the university were invited to participate as speakers and resource persons for these workshops.

After several years of conducting these workshops on the university campus, it was decided to experiment with the idea of promoting and sponsoring workshops in the various local communities in conjunction with a neighborhood organization, affiliated with the Commission on Delinquency Prevention. This added local program resulted in greater participation by local communities in youth welfare activities for delinquency prevention and rehabilitation of juvenile delinquents.

It is very important for the community worker and members of the committee to understand that conditions being experienced in various communities today make this a propitious time to enlist the services of the local colleges and universities in helping to resolve some of the existing social problems. Faculty members and students are anxious to be of service "where the action is," and the neighborhood committee through the worker and membership can be instrumental in "bringing the university to the community" in an effort to alleviate social problems.

However, this too serves as an auxiliary resource similar to business interest, labor support, and the like, and should be integrated into the overall comprehensive community program and not looked on as a simple solution to a complex problem.

Still other efforts that staff and related volunteers can initiate to improve in-depth awareness and understanding of the neighborhood program by various publics is through a good working relationship with the newspapers and other media of communication.

A vital aspect in dealing with the news media is a planned effort to establish and maintain rapport that results in a sympathetic relationship rather than a skeptical or even antagonistic attitude.

Often the news media obtain an item in an incomplete or unilateral form. For a variety of reasons, which might range from ignorance about a source of authorized information all the way to a lack of confidence, such an item could be published without verification of essential details to the detriment of entire programs.

Therefore, it is urgent that a regular relationship be established with the editors so the worker is contacted about any news items, positive or negative, to give the worker an opportunity to verify, amplify, temper, or refute the items. To create this atmosphere the worker, of course, must have earned the respect and gratitude of the media by acting as a regular source of legitimate and accurate material.

Chapter 4

WORKING WITH YOUNG PEOPLE

Neighborhood committees can provide services for children from many different types of facilities. Many communities in Chicago operate out of rented storefront centers and several groups have purchased their own buildings. Others have rent-free space in housing projects, churches, and even police stations. In addition to the headquarters or centers out of which they operate, many committees have been resourceful in arranging available space in schools, churches, housing projects, and public parks, always by special arrangement with these institutions, of course.

Storefront centers or small buildings have certain advantages. They are located closer to the people where the problems exist. They are funded, managed, and operated by local residents, and also, because they symbolize the residents' interests and leadership, storefront centers or small buildings are likely to exercise greater influence and have more significance in the lives of the people than some of the large, superimposed, outside agencies. It is interesting to note that during the past decade many social agencies have discontinued operating settlement houses or community centers and have opened storefront centers. Even some law enforcement agencies have experimented with this approach. Police departments, city agencies, and a variety of federally or state funded poverty projects have decided that there could be better delivery of their services at the grass-roots level by maintaining storefront centers. However, there is still more merit in the centers operated by neighborhood committees since they embody the principle of self-help. They are financed by local residents and are under their management and leadership.

The storefront centers operated by neighborhood committees are used for children's activities as well as meeting places for teenagers and adults, for parties, and for other special occasions. In addition to counseling children in trouble or families confronted with problems, these centers usually provide such activities as game rooms, Scouting, artwork, handicrafts, sewing, and other social and recreational programs under the leadership of volunteers and paid workers.

Any area chosen as a playground or recreational area should be large enough and equipped to accommodate as many activities at one time, serving the needs and interests of neighborhood residents.

Before actually providing programming for youngsters, there should be available responsible, trained leaders; junior leaders; and other supportive personnel. When a neighborhood committee decides to organize a recreational program, it should first seek out interested individuals in the neighborhood who will be willing to devote the time necessary to make these programs work. Consideration should also be given to structuring the program so that time segments will be appropriate to enable volunteers to contribute their time, to methods of approaching the youngsters under discussion, to the best available location for a recreational program, and to ways of obtaining equipment or funds for the program.

Probably the biggest need will be in obtaining a meeting place for youngsters. In addition to the committee's own center, the following are suggested places.

1. *School Playground.* Probably the most logical place would be on a school playground; this is especially true in the summer months when this area may be relatively underutilzed. Permission for its use should be obtained from the local school authorites. Usually the playground will be large enough to accommodate activities for several age groups at the same time. A schedule should be drawn up so that all groups will have opportunities to use the available facilities. This factor is true for any area that would be chosen as a recreational center.

2. *Empty Lots.* If a school playground is not available, or if it is not large enough to accommodate all groups, another place that may be used is an empty lot in the neighborhood. For this, it would be necessary to obtain permission of the owner. Since it would very likely be unsuitable for use because of trash, weeds, or other accumulations, it would provide a good civic project to clean up the lot for use by the children. Young and old alike could participate in this project, serving as a unifying force for the community. Community efforts could be continued by joining together to make articles and equipment for the youngsters, for example, sandboxes, slides, simple jungle gyms, basketball ring, baseball diamond, horseshoe pit, and many other objects.

3. *Local Church Yard or Parking Lot.* In this situation, the group would have to be careful in selecting a location. Permission should be granted by the pastor and/or board of elders of the church. Some churches do not

allow dancing or playing in the area of the church. The committee must also avoid being accused of favoritism and see that the church group does not try to control the program.

4. *Side Streets.* If the situation is such that none of the above places are available, especially in large cities where space is at a premium, a small side street might be blocked off for a few hours each day for a recreational program. Problems arising with the setting up of this program would have to be worked out with the Traffic Department of the city in question.

5. *Field Houses.* Another possibility might be a field house, which is usually large enough to accommodate many groups and many activities at the same time. Arrangements for its use should be made with the appropriate authorities (school board, park district, housing project).

VOLUNTEERS TO SERVE

After recognizing a definite need for a recreational activity and deciding where to set up facilities, a community worker can try to get the participation and help of various individuals and groups throughout the community. Besides organizing, conducting, and financing the program, volunteers can bring much enthusiasm, recognition, and appreciation to the program as a whole. It must be determined who can serve as volunteers, how they can be reached, and what they can do.

Volunteers can be obtained from many sources. Parents in the community are the most important of these sources. Their cooperation and involvement in the recreational program can mean a much more successful outcome. Parents can be reached individually or as a group. Groups such as the P.T.A., block parents, and various neighborhood and community groups involving parents can be useful as sponsors for projects. Young people can be of great help as junior leaders and all-around helpers. They can be recruited from high school clubs, student councils, church and synagogue groups, Sunday Schools, 4-H Clubs, Boy Scouts, and Girl Scouts. Volunteers can be recruited throughout the community and from other civic organizations, various church groups, and even the clergy. In addition, volunteers can be obtained from various neighborhood associations such as tenants' groups, improvement associations, and dramatic and musical clubs.

Many community groups such as veterans' associations, lodges, fraternal organizations, labor unions, women's auxiliaries, hobby clubs, and the like can serve as sponsors. Even some neighborhood newspapers, radio stations, advertising clubs, and shopping plazas might serve as sponsors.

Person-to-person contact is probably one of the most effective methods for obtaining volunteers, and this can take place almost anywhere: individual homes, business offices, and youth "hangouts." Other methods that can be used are direct mail, telephone, and informal talks before various groups.

There are many things volunteers can do. (1) They can organize an initial operating committee and develop step-by-step plans for carrying out the projects. (2) They can obtain, especially in the case of sponsor groups, money and equipment for the program. Children of suitable ages can be recruited as volunteers. (3) Volunteers can lead, guide, and instruct the recreational program itself. (4) They can also evaluate the program, make adjustments, and arrange for the progression of and the expansion of the program in the future.

ACTIVITIES

We have prepared Tables 4.1 to 4.3 listing activities for age groups from 7 to 17. Some of the activities can also be used with

Table 4.1 Sports Activities

Activity	Age	Place	Cost	Advisability	Need of supervision
Archery	10–17	Open field	Expensive because of equipment	Only if adequate funds available	Instructor should be present at beginning
Badminton	7–17	Any moderately open area	Inexpensive—need birdie and racket	Good activity for youngsters	Need very little—only to learn rules
Baseball	7–17	Field	Inexpensive—need bat, mitts, and ball; expensive if uniforms are needed	Very good activity	Coaches and referees
Basketball	8–17	Basketball court	Inexpensive—only need ball and rim	Very good activity	Coaches and referees
Bowling	7–17	Bowling alley	Rather expensive	Only if a good rate is obtained	Little after rules and scoring are learned
Boxing	7–17	Gym or field house	Moderate—need mats and gloves	Good for building muscles	Much supervision
Croquet	7–17	Moderately open area	Moderate to expensive, depending on materials	Good for coordination and judgment	Only to teach rules
Golf	10–17	Golf course	Expensive	Poor because of cost and fees	Little on links
Hockey	10–17	Ice or open flat area	Inexpensive to expensive	Poor because of limited area	Great supervision
Horseshoes	7–17	Horseshoe pit	Inexpensive	Good activity	Little

Table 4.1 (Continued)

Obstacle race	7–17	Large open area	Inexpensive	Good—helps build body and team play	Coaches and judges
Ping-Pong	7–17	Recreation center	Inexpensive	Good activity	Very little
Running matches	7–17	Open area	Inexpensive	Good for coordination	Only coaches
Shuffleboard	7–17	Small open area	Moderate expense	Good as a variety activity	Little
Skating—ice and roller	7–17	Ice or roller rink	Ice: cost of skates Roller: skates and admission fee	Good for coordination; not advised if rates not given by rink	Moderate
Softball	7–17	Open field	Inexpensive—need bat and ball	Very good activity	Coaches and umpires
Swimming	7–17	Pool	Inexpensive	Good activity	Much supervision
Tennis	10–17	Tennis court	Inexpensive—ball and racket	Good activity	Little after rules are learned
Tobogganing	7–17	Small hill (7–13); steeper slopes for older groups (14–17)	Inexpensive	Good winter sport	Much supervision for younger children
Volleyball	10–17	Any moderately open area	Inexpensive	Good mixer activity	Little
Wrestling	10–17	Gym	Inexpensive—need mats	Good for building muscles	Much supervision

Table 4.2 Outdoor Activities Other Than Sports

Activity	Age	Place	Cost	Advisability	Need of supervision
Bird study	7–17	Open area, country	Inexpensive	Depends on interest of youngsters	One who knows about birds
Camping	7–17	Campgrounds	Inexpensive	Good if able to obtain materials	Much supervision
Collecting nature specimens	7–17	Country or campgrounds	Moderate	Good for learning about nature	Moderate
Hiking	7–17	Country or campgrounds	Inexpensive	Very good activity	Much supervision
Picnics	7–17	Country or campgrounds	Inexpensive	Good mixer activity	Little
Star study	7–17	Country, or anywhere stars can be seen	Inexpensive	Depends on interest of youngsters	One who knows about stars and constellations
Scavenger hunt	7–17	Anywhere	No cost	Good mixer activity	Little
Hayride	13–17	Country	Rental of horse and wagon	Very good mixer activity	Little
Tree study	7–17	Country is best	Inexpensive	Depends on interest of youngsters	One who knows about trees

Table 4.3 Crafts and Skills

Activity	Age	Place	Cost	Advisability	Need of supervision
Basketry	7–17	Recreation center	Moderate expense to the center	Good activity	Moderate to little, once mastered
Block printing	7–17	Recreation center	Inexpensive—need potato or eraser	Good activity	Little, once learned
Carpentry	12–17	Shop in recreation center	Tools for the shop	Good skill, but should be done in recreation center	Much supervision
Cooking	12–17	Recreation center kitchen	Moderate to expensive	Should be learned, but done in recreation center	Much supervision
Finger painting	7–10	Recreation center	Inexpensive	Good activity	Little
Home decorating	12–17	Recreation center	Can be expensive	Should be conducted in recreation center for a fee	Moderate
Leather work	7–17	Recreation center	Moderate to expensive	Good as craft or skill; because of expense should be done in recreation center	Moderate supervision

Table 4.3 (Continued)

Activity	Age	Place	Cost	Advisability	Need of supervision
Painting	7–17	Recreation center	Expensive	Good to broaden activities and develop skills	A good teacher
Photography	10–17	Recreation center	Expensive	Good skill, but too expensive	A good teacher
Poster making	12–17	Recreation center or homes	Rather inexpensive	Good; helps with advertising other projects	Moderate
Soap carving	7–17	Recreation center	Inexpensive	Good skill	Much for younger children
Printing	14–17	Recreation center	Expensive	Learning process as well as activity; should be in a recreation center	Much supervision
Sewing	12–17	Recreation center	Moderate to expensive	Good; should be in recreation center	Much supervision for beginners
Wood carving	12–17	Recreation center	Moderate expense for the center	Good as skill and learning activity	Much supervision

younger children, but only the 7-to-17 group is considered in this chapter.

The activities listed in the crafts section should be conducted in a community center for the most successful results. The cost and advisability columns for the crafts section are based on the premise that the community center would be able to supply the required materials at a minimum fee to the youngsters. If this is not the case, then the cost would be great and, therefore, would probably change the practicality of some projects.

Some outdoor activities would depend greatly for success on the interests and development of the youngsters involved.

There are many excellent programs that can be used to fit other leisure time needs. These provide already established programs, books and equipment, and even leadership training. Existing clubs and organizations should be considered as sources since they can help make the organizing and programming easier and more productive.

Following the tables is a list of other activities that could be conducted in a recreation program, especially if it is conducted in a community center. These are merely outline suggestions. Each neighborhood—its needs and its potential resources (in people, money, membership)—must be evaluated individually and a realistic program developed that is workable and appropriate.

Success is a vital ingredient for community organization. Additional recreation features can be added to an ongoing program, but the overly ambitious program that cannot be sustained not only deprives the young people of a needed service, but also serves as "burnt-over territory," that is, as an impediment for future more practical efforts. Therefore, be sure you plan your work so you can work your plan.

Following is a list of activities that can be conducted in a recreational program, especially if the program is conducted in a recreational center.

Dramatic: Acting, charades, puppet shows, making scenery, marionettes, minstrel shows, producing and directing plays, reading plays, shadow puppets, stage lighting, theatrical makeup, writing plays.

Social: Banquets, dances, dance classes, folk dancing, parties.

Musical: Bugle, fife, and drum corps, chorus or choir, creative songwriting, folk songs, glee clubs, music appreciation, listening group, playing in band or orchestra, singing in operetta.

Literary: Book club, current events club, debating, discussions and forums, "Information Please," quiz programs.

Table games: Backgammon, bingo, bridge, cards, checkers, chess, dominoes, paper-and-pencil games, making airplane models.

Civilian services: Act as hospital aides, help Red Cross, renovate furniture and home equipment, help harvest crops, collect scrap, paper, etc., act as playground aides, act as aides in child care centers, help committees, act as library assistants, make nature exhibits for child care centers, survey neighborhoods, write letters to neighbors away from home.

An excellent 36-page brochure, *A Guide To Books On Recreation,* is a bibliography compiled expressly for professional and volunteer recreation and park workers and all others interested in recreation in any setting. This bibliography is an authoritative source for literature dealing with all phases of recreation and parks. The extensive listings cover the following subjects: Arts, crafts, and hobbies; music and dance; drama, puppetry, and storytelling; sports and athletics; games; nature and outing activities; social recreation; areas, facilities, and equipment; holiday activities; and professional development. This brochure may be obtained from the National Recreation & Park Association, 1700 Pennsylvania Avenue, N.W., Washington, D.C. 20006.

Chapter 5

FUNDRAISING IN THE COMMUNITY

NEED FOR FUNDS

A very important and immediate problem facing a newly formed committee is the need for funds to carry on its program. Funds may be needed for rented offices, furniture, electricity, telephone, stationery, postage, and so on. These are only a few of the items that will face an organization in the beginning and, with time, as the program is developed, there will be a greater need for funds. In keeping with the goal to make each neighborhood committee self-sustaining, the committee members will have to devise various means to meet their basic financial needs (Flanagan, 1977).

The extent of the programs that a neighborhood committee feels it needs and desires will determine the size of its operating budget. The committee should establish a priority for its programs and determine the amount of funding required. In this way, by doing first things first, the committee will be able to begin its vital programs and then extend its services as the ability to finance is expanded.

Funds are needed to provide the kind of programs that will offer youths more constructive ways to channel their energies and utilize their talents and ideas. Such activities as handicrafts, athletics, social activities, and outdoor programs may be used as a means to attract youth for the more specialized services such as guidance, assistance in securing employment, cultural enlightenment, tutoring, student aid, attention for dropouts, and any counseling when a difficulty arises.

The amount of money needed depends on such factors as volume of service anticipated, number and kinds of activities and programs planned, number of people to be served, and the extent and availability of facilities and resources. When the volunteer staff is assisted by paid personnel, hired by the neighborhood committee, it is obvious that there will be an even greater need for funds.

It is difficult to separate the development of fundraising projects from the programs and activities planned for the youth. It is important for the neighborhood committee to set up short-range as well as long-range plans as a way to save money in programming, fundraising, or any other activity. Budgets should be planned on a yearly basis to help the members better understand their responsibilities to the committee and the youth they serve.

Factors Affecting Success of Fundraising Campaigns

A fundraising campaign is actually a sales and public relations program. In approaching the potential contributor, charity should not be the goal of the solicitation; it is the program and what it will do for the community and how it will benefit youth (and particularly the individual members) that should be stressed. Every attempt should be made to show how the contribution may affect the contributor in a positive manner. The initial approach should be a brief appeal to the emotions of the contributor, indicating the goals to be achieved and how these will assist both individuals in need and the community as a whole.

Every neighborhood committee should state its case to the community in such a way to gain as much support and acceptance as possible. The appeal for funds should take place over a sustained period of time and not merely be turned on like a tap at a time the organization needs money. The approach must be clear and easily understood by the average citizen. The need for the committee's services must be clearly established, and it should be shown that it is capable of carrying out the programs for which funds are being sought.

To be successful, a fundraising program for any agency must conform to certain established principles and procedures. Their application will vary according to the size and scope of the organization. The following factors require serious consideration.

1. *Realistic Goals.* General goals do *not* obtain contributions. It is better to select a series of small specific goals. A fundraising project should be selected that is assured of success. By setting a realistic goal, the committee members will work hard to achieve it, since success will be within their grasp.

2. *Planning the Campaign.* This is a basic requirement for every organization. A policy statement containing the scope of the committee's activities should be developed. Within this policy, the campaign structure should be developed, outlining the areas of fundraising. A specific period should be designated for a concentrated campaign, and then the major resources of the committee should be directed toward this effort. The responsibilities of each participant should be outlined in detail so that each understands his or her part in the overall program. A time schedule should be thought out in advance long before the campaign kickoff and include deadlines—deadlines for recruiting a captain, for recruiting workers, for obtaining prospect lists, for calling on potential contributors, for turning in receipts, and the like.

3. *Leadership.* The best-laid plans are worthless without an enthusiastic, well-informed group of volunteers. There must be sufficient leaders willing to accept responsibility, and they must have substantial influence in order to attract gifts and inspire workers. A "5 by 5 by 5" ratio is important. This means that the captain would have approximately five lieutenants who would have approximately five sergeants, and so on, until a comprehensive organization would be structured for calling on potential contributors.

4. *Recruitment and Use of Workers.* Face-to-face solicitation of one person to another is the best approach in fundraising. Therefore, the committee must plan to recruit volunteers as workers on a scale sufficient to cover the area of personal solicitation. The established members of the committee must actively participate in the fundraising program and, by their example, stimulate enthusiasm and support from outsiders.

5. *Publicity.* A neighborhood committee raising funds must have policies and methods of fundraising that are acceptable to the public to which it is appealing. The publicity program should be constant and should continue even after the fundraising campaign has ended. Contributors should be kept informed of what is being done with their money. Keeping the community informed of their activities and accomplishments should be a year-round effort.

6. *Fundraising Budget.* This should be established as soon as the campaign plan is completed. Costs of each phase of the campaign should be measured with the potential of that particular phase. Personal solicitation is the most productive form of fundraising and probably the least expensive. Costs for larger campaigns run from 4 to 8 percent. Smaller campaigns invariably cost more. In any case, the cost should not exceed 15 percent of the amount raised. If it does, the board should conduct a thorough review to determine where economies can be made.

7. *Suitable Dates.* The date of a fundraising project or campaign is important to consider if it is to be successful.

Scheduling an event too close to a major holiday or in competition with other events such as a church social in the community can be disastrous as far as attendance is concerned.

8.   *Records.* It is important to maintain records on the development of the campaign plan, its execution, and ultimate results. A list of potential and actual contributors should be maintained. During the course of the year, outside the campaign, publicity attempts should be made to send printed material to these individuals apprising them of the current activities. It is a sound policy not to restrict the contacts to the time when contributions are desired.

9.   *Accounting.* The fundraising committee should always keep accurate accounting records and issue up-to-date treasury reports. All money should be accounted for. Usually, where a product is not involved, a receipt should be issued to the contributor with a carbon retained for the committee's record. It is ideal to have a duplicate receipt for all monies received. All paid expenses should be substantiated by an invoice, check, or other documentary proof. The final proceeds of any event should be audited by a group of officers or members of the committee. These reports should be circulated so that every member is aware of the financial situation.

10.   *Final Results.* A too-often-neglected step is an announcement of the results of the campaign accompanied by an appreciative statement.

SELF-EVALUATION

Each fundraising project should be carefully scrutinized and evaluated. This evaluation should cover all phases of the fundraising campaign to determine the weak and strong areas. Those projects that produced good results within reasonable expense limitations should be included in future plans. Projects that did not produce desirable results should be reviewed and, if possible, corrective measures recommended. Otherwise, these should be discarded in future plans.

In making a self-evaluation, the following points should be reviewed:

1. Were the goals realistic?
2. What deficiencies were noted in the planned campaign? How could it have been improved?
3. Did the leadership meet the challenge of the campaign?
4. Was the recruitment and use of volunteers adequate?
5. Was the publicity sufficient to arouse the public and get the workers to be active?
6. Was the fundraising budget appropriate and did it meet the needs of the campaign?
7. Were the dates in conflict with other events?
8. How can the list of potential contributors be enlarged?
9. Did the accounting records provide accurate financial reports?
10. How much income were you *budgeted to* raise?
11. How much did you *actually* raise?
12. How does the amount raised this year compare with last year?
13. About what percentage of this year's amount, if any, was from new contributors?
14. What percent of your contribution income represented expenses for your campaign?

If the number of new contributors is 5 percent or less, more effort should be devoted to expanding the campaign to cover areas not now being solicited. Normally, 3 percent of previous contributors are lost due to deaths, removal from the area, and other causes.

The large variety of fundraising projects will require a flexible approach in carrying out the campaign and in its ultimate evaluation. The general principles will apply to a great extent, although there may be variations in the degree of application.

SUGGESTED FUNDRAISING PROJECTS

A large variety of fundraising projects may be utilized by the neighborhood committee. It will be up to the committee to decide which one best fits their situation. Following is a number of potential fundraising projects, although it is not all inclusive.

1. *Private or Public Funding*

   In some communities it may be possible for the members to obtain funds for well-structured programs from private philanthropic organizations; local, state, and federal agencies; or community chests. Usually a comprehensive written plan must be presented, giving in detail the objectives of the program, means of execution, and a total breakdown of the expected expenses. In some instances there may be a provision for the matching funds. Since the preparation of the proposal is of a technical nature, requiring certain specific skills, it is best to seek assistance from individuals who have experience in this area.

2. *Direct Solicitation*

   (a) Make up a list of potential donors, such as local merchants, professionals, and the like. Such a list must be rated by the committee to determine a reasonable potential contribution for each donor.

   (b) Set up three-by-five cards listing potential contributors, and distribute these cards to members who will do the soliciting. Quotas are an important part of fundraising. If a worker gets five cards with a committee appraisal of $30, he or she should strive to meet this quota.

   (c) Set a deadline for all solicitation to be completed.

   (d) Issue a receipt to each contributor.

   (e) Send a thank-you letter to donors of a contribution over a set amount.

(f) Use the money raised for the expressed purpose for which it was intended.

(g) Publicize the amount raised and its use.

3. *Carnival or Festival*

(a) Select a "live wire" site extending over an area three blocks or a large vacant lot. Select a date.

(b) Get permission for holding the event from local officials. Permission may include four or five permits such as streets, fire, food, mechanical rides, neighbors, and so on.

(c) Select a bona fide carnival-supply dealer. Work out a fair-money sharing arrangement. The dealer should provide all rides, booths, games, and so on, which must be legitimate. Check for accident insurance coverage.

(d) Organize a committee of volunteers who will run the rides, booths, games, and the like, where it is safe for amateurs to do so.

(e) Put in some innovations of your own, such as special food stands, entertainment, prizes, special games, kiddie matinees, amateur nights, and so on.

(f) Give the event sufficient publicity.

(g) Make the event appealing and fun for the entire family.

(h) Solicit the help of other community organizations to increase participation and support.

(i) Provide for police protection, first aid, money storage arrangements, and insurance.

4. *Family Picnic*

(a) Select a convenient picnic grove. This can be in the county forest preserve or a private grove.

(b) Get permission to use the picnic grove. In larger cities this may have to be done 6 to 8 months in advance for a good area.

(c) Publicize the event.

(d) Organize games and other entertainment for children and adults.

(e) Provide refreshments.

(f) Organize transportation if needed.

(g) Provide controls over money and sales to eliminate freeloading.

Note: On some public grounds no food or beverages can be sold. If, however, an all-inclusive ticket is sold in advance of the affair, with the ticket reading "Good for one *dinner* and program at X Y Z picnic," without a price affixed to it, there may be no objection. Note also any local ordinance or regulations restricting the consumption of alcoholic beverages on the premises. Make sure that any such rules are enforced.

5. *Spaghetti Dinner, Chili Supper, Corn Boil, Fish Fry, Pancake Lunch*

(a) Obtain use of an adequate facility such as local church, school, community center, and the like.

(b) Set the date of the event.

(c) Set a price.

(d) Purchase food and beverages. (Try to get donations whenever possible.)

(e) Get cooks, waiters or waitresses, dishwashers, and so on, from the community.

(f) Advertise the event.

(g) Provide additional innovations such as entertainment, group singing, "carry-out" orders, and so on.

(h) If the facility belongs to another organization, be sure it is left clean, including equipment, cooking utensils, silverware, china, glasses, waste disposal, wardrobe, and the outside entrance to the building.

6. *Business and Industry Luncheon*

This is an excellent way to raise funds if your group is located in a neighborhood with industry and a variety of business firms, both retail and wholesale. A good time to hold it is 12:30 P.M.

(a) Make up a list of potential guests (industry and business firms in the community).

(b) Set a date and time for the luncheon.

(c) Have several prominent businesspeople of the area (someone who is already "sold" on your committee's work and goals, etc.) send letters to people on this list.

(d) Follow up by personal phone calls.

(e) If at all possible, try to have the luncheon in your own headquarters, youth center, hall, or office, and try to get local *volunteers* to cook and serve the luncheon. The charge may be about $10 to $15 per person. However, some committees do not charge but later follow up with an appeal for a contribution, either at the luncheon or at a later date.

(f) Set up a brief, interesting program. Know exactly what you are going to do and say and when. For the charge involved you should provide a really good program.

(g) Get through on time (e.g., by 2 P.M.). Remember these are busy people, and they have other important things to do.

(h) Get your message across: why you need the money, and what you intend to do with it. Be specific. For example, you need $150 for softball, baseball, and athletic supplies to take care of 200 children for the coming summer.

You need $150 to send 20 boys and girls to summer camp for a one-week period. You need $100 to take 150 children to see big league baseball and other major sports. You need $100 for records, supplies, refreshments and so on, for a teenage canteen for 100 teenagers who meet twice a week.

(i) Be sure you give each donor a receipt for his or her gift.

(j) Be sure you send each donor a thank-you letter.

(k) Be sure to use the money for the purpose intended.

(l) Invite them again next year.

7. *Annual Fundraising Dinner*

This affair can be used to combine the essence of an annual meeting with the added important element of raising money. This may be held as a moderate, medium, or large-scale affair depending on your committee's potential, experience, budget, size of membership, and willingness to work. To give it added attraction, the following may be included: use of speaker, entertainment, prizes, or after-dinner dancing. It is essential that the *menu* be both appetizing and appealing, and that it provide the guests all the food they want! More important than food is a *brief, proper, good* program.

For smaller goals such as $1000 to $3000, a set fee may be charged—perhaps $10 per person. However, for a much larger goal, such as $4000 to $8000, no fee is charged; the guest gives according to his or her ability and according to the dictates of his or her heart. In the latter case, it is important to note that all guests who plan to attend this kind of affair are "warned" ahead of time with regard to the *generous* contribution they will be expected to give, thereby avoiding embarrassment to the guests and financial loss to the fundraising event. Again, to give added assurance of success to this kind of endeavor, it is much better to hold it in your own facility, with volunteer waiters and waitresses. This provides the right setting, assuring you of better service and inviting a better response.

8. *Using a Souvenir Program Book*

This may be used as an additional money-raising tool to your major dinner, banquet, carnival, bazaar, luncheon, or other program.

(a) Ads are solicited from businesspeople, politicians, merchants, churches, doctors, lawyers, and so on. Care should be exercised in the kinds of ads solicited.

(b) Ads are sold by size of page—one-eighth, one-fourth, one-half, three-quarters, and full page.

(c) Prices may range from $2.50 for a one-eighth page to $25 for a full page, or from $5 for an one-eighth page to $50 for a full page.

(d) Pictures of activities and news stories of the committee's work are excellent ways to promote ad sales.

(e) Persons may advertise their place of business, or just extend their good wishes to the committee.

(f) The average method is to have about 750 to 1000 books printed and distributed to members, advertisers, and to the general community.

(g) The advertiser must feel that the book is actually going to advertise him or her. Therefore, the distribution figure *must* be honest. If 1000 are printed, then 1000 must be given out or you are cheating the advertiser—and he or she will soon know it and refuse to donate under the guise of advertising.

(h) This can become an annual affair and can grow from year to year.

Another number of potential fundraising projects requiring varying degrees of membership participation is given in the following list. Although no operational guidelines are given for these suggestions, it would be well for the committee to review the organizational recommendations utilized in the first eight projects listed above.

1. *Household Needs.* Selling of such useful items as light bulbs, polish, cleaner, and the like. (*Note:* Do not infringe upon any other civic organization's established fundraising methods by selling the same or competitive products in the same community.)

2. *King or Queen for Teenage Clubs.* Candidates are chosen who sell popularity votes at 1 cent each. The one bringing in the most money is crowned king or queen at a party or dance.

3. *Hayrides.* A destination is chosen in the country. A fee is charged for transportation that may or may not include the price of refreshments. If not, simple food such as hot dogs or hamburgers are sold at the destination.

4. *Traveling Basket.* A sealed container for money, with a list of those to whom the basket is to travel, is placed in a basket, usually by the club president, who starts the basket on its travels and takes it to the first name on the list. That person removes the gift, puts as much money in the container as he or she thinks it is worth (not less than 50 cents) replaces it with another gift, and takes it to the next person on the list. The basket ends with the one who started it, who keeps the last gift.

5. *Silver Teas.* The host or organization sends out invitations in whatever way seems best: newspapers, club bulletin, and the like. A beautifully appointed tea table comprised of little cakes, mints, and nuts, and tea and coffee is provided. A small silver tray or pretty plate is placed in a conspicuous place at the door or on the table where the guests are expected to place silver coins in payment for the tea. These are very nice social affairs.

6. *Antique Exhibits.* Every town has many pieces of antique furniture, old glass, quilts, and other relics that the owners are happy to lend for showing. A style show of old wedding

gowns may be combined as part of the show. Admission is charged.

7. *Doughnut or Pie Sales.* Homemade pies, warm from the oven, may be sold from a truck rather than a store.

8. *Homemade Cupcakes Sale.* Thirty-two women in one committee worked 2 months baking and boxing 1200 cakes that were placed in freezers until the date of the well-publicized sale. They made $200.

9. *Seven-Table Feast.* This is another version of a church dinner. Seven tables are set up and used as buffets from which the menu is served. One table is covered in green and from this is served the green vegetables and salads. From a white table, bread and rolls are served; from a yellow table, pastry; a brown table, roast beef and chicken; yellow table no. 2, cheese and macaroni and potato salad; a red table, beets, and brown table no. 2, coffee and tea. A volunteer stands at each table and serves.

10. *Earn a Dollar.* Each member of a club or organization pledges to earn a dollar. Wives cannot accept money from husbands or vice versa unless some special service is performed for which the spouse would normally pay someone else. At the meeting at which the money is turned in, all must tell how they earned their dollars. This is loads of fun.

11. *50/50 Club.* This is financed by the selling of tickets. Half of the proceeds go to the club or committee and the other half goes to the holder of ticket drawn from drum.

12. *Country Store.* This is the sale of items such as garden produce, fresh fruit, flowers, and perhaps grain; this could include seeds. Other items to be sold might include home-canned vegetables and fruits and fresh, cured, or canned meat, as well as home-baked items.

13. *Raffle Party.* Select a series of items for which persons may buy chances. Arrangements should be made to have local merchants donate the merchandise to be raffled; or members might donate books of trading stamps to obtain items for the raffle. It is difficult to publicize lotteries, raffles, or door prizes since it is illegal for newspapers to publish references to such events.

14. *Supper Club Varieties.* A variety of foods such as box lunches are bid on by people in attendance.

15. Sale of vanilla, stationery, and greeting cards and candy or nuts—boxed, tinned, or homemade.

16. Street dances, home talent plays, and style shows.

17. Collection of waste paper. Check the market first. It may not pay for the effort at certain times.

18. Country bazaars or benefit movies.

19. Snow cone machine, popcorn machine, or food stand at parks, fairs, or shopping centers.

20. Card parties and auctions.

21. Older children might bathe and groom dogs, or perhaps offer a dog-walking service.

22. Youngsters doing odd jobs—money earned to be donated to the project.

23. Band concert—free-will offering.

24. Amateur hour with participants paying small entrance fee; prizes to be donated.

25. Sale of holly wreaths on Christmas trees. Some organizations raise their own trees for this purpose.

26. Community car wash.

27. Rummage, bargain, white elephant, or next-to-new sales.

28. *Social Game Parties.* A fee is charged for various games taken part in such as donkey tail pinning, and so on.

29. *Shoe Size or Tape Measure Dance.* Price of admission to dance is based on size of shoe: 5 cents per size. Admission to tape measure dance is figured at 1 cent per inch around waist or height.

These projects are examples that can be used, although the resourcefulness of the members of the neighborhood committee will no doubt originate other methods of raising funds.

Chapter 6

THE EXPERIENCE OF
REHABILITATION

How Neighbors Assist

Experiences of neighborhood committees show that the rehabilitation of the delinquent can be achieved by incorporating the delinquent into conventional social groupings of citizens in the neighborhood. Whether the delinquent continues in delinquency or in some legitimate activity depends to a very large extent on the attitudes the delinquent encounters among his or her neighbors. If the delinquent is regarded as an ex-convict and ostracized from conventional groupings, it is very probable that he or she will continue in crime. In those districts where neighborhood committees of local residents have made a systematic effort to incorporate delinquents and parolees into conventional groups, the probabilities of rehabilitation have been greatly increased. Neighborhood residents accomplished this simply by aiding and encouraging the offender to participate and to become identified with the persons and the activities of the committee or similar neighborhood organizations. By this means, the parolee establishes new personal relationships with the neighbors and in time achieves a position of responsibility and respectability in the community.

This process of rehabilitation is illustrated by the following excerpt from an interview with a parolee:

> . . . I was paroled from Pontiac after doing about three years. My sponsor was an organization downtown. I would just bring my paper (monthly report) up and they would sign it and I would take it up once a month. They would never check or see me during the month. They didn't care about me. Nobody cared about me. I was supposed to have a job. As soon as I went to work and said I was an ex-con, the job went boom. They didn't want me so I just walked the streets and got back with the old gang. For ten months I was out robbing and burglarizing before I got caught. We got the rap for everything that was stolen in the community. . . . I was sent to Joliet. I was in Joliet for nine years. . . .
>
> I had just about given up hopes of ever getting out when my sister told me that a couple of members of the community committee were interested in helping me. When they appeared in my behalf and things looked pretty favorable, I was given a new lease on life because someone was fighting for me who didn't always remind me that I had served time. Finally, I was paroled to the committee and they got me a job with a local company.
>
> It sure gives a man a new lease on life knowing that somebody will be interested in him, help him get a job, get him interested in sports, and other activities. When I got out everyone treated me like an old friend. If I had any problems, some of the members of the committee would always give me a helping hand . . .
>
> Whenever I needed money, I could borrow it from some of the committee. I wasn't ashamed to ask for it. I made up my mind to go straight as long as I had a few friends who could discuss my problems with me.
>
> . . . Since I've been paroled, I spent a lot of my time in the club, operated by the committee, helping with the program. It gives a person a feeling that he is doing something worthwhile.

Two Young Men

Here are two former offenders who were born and raised on the Near West Side of Chicago. These two stories written in the

1950s illustrate how offenders make a transition from crime to conventional life. As Mario indicates in this first story he wrote, as soon as he was released from prison, he became actively involved in the Near West Side Community Committee and served as a volunteer and member of the Board of Directors for several decades. The second story is by James, a middle-aged man who spent approximately 20 years in the various branches of the Illinois State Penitentiary. He was visited by a member of the Committee while he was in the institution, aided in securing parole and when he was released, he was assisted with employment and welcomed into the group. He has been a valuable volunteer, served on various subcommittees and on the Board of Directors of the Community Committee.

Mario

I'm going to skip all the details of prison life and come to the day when I came out. What a day! The outside looked so different. I don't know how to describe it but you feel you are in a different world. Everything looks strange at first—and you feel glad in a way that you are out and then you wonder—What now? I had no plans or ideas of my future. I just didn't know what I was going to do or to whom I would turn.

I was lucky that when I came out of prison, my sister and her husband asked me to live with them. They spent a lot of money for doctor's care for me. I was physically run down and had to go to a family doctor for about six months getting shots and vitamins. The 5 years in prison had not agreed with me. I was fussy about what I ate, but there was no choice, you ate what they gave you or starved.

I had a big ten dollar bill when I came out and a suit of clothes that made you very self-conscious. Anybody that had any experience with prison would know where you came from by looking at you. The clothes were a dead give away. My sister helped me by buying some new clothes and after this I went out to try to find a job. Since I had served the full time I was out on a discharge and not parole and hence I did not need a job as a condition of my release.

When I went looking for a job and I was asked to fill out an application blank there was the question I was afraid would be put to me. "Ever been arrested and if so give details." I figured I might as well tell the truth because if they found out later it would be worse. Of course I was told there was nothing doing and I left wondering what my next step was going to be.

The next day I was walking down Polk Street and I see a storefront fixed like an office and the sign read WEST SIDE COMMUNITY COMMITTEE. There I saw Tony Sorrentino, who used to hang out on my street and I went in to see him. There were other fellows around that I knew and we started talking. They knew of course where I had been but not when I came out. They seemed to be interested in helping because they asked me if I wanted a job and maybe they could help. So I told them then that I was turned down for a job because of my record.

After Tony and Joe Giunta asked me further questions they got in a car and went to see the employment manager of the firm. Whatever they told him must have made a hit because when they came back they said I could go back to the firm and that I would be hired. All they wanted to offer me was thirty cents an hour and I couldn't see how I could live on $12 or so a week so I refused it.

The Committee helped me by giving a few dollars for carfare, for cigarettes, and for a movie. From this time on my social life was built around the Committee. In fact, it's been this way all the years since I came out of prison.

The first year I was home from prison, I had about eight different jobs, but they were not in my trade and I didn't like any of them. Part of my trouble in getting a job in my trade was that I could not show the employment manager my diploma since it showed the branch of the state prison and was signed by the prison warden. Some diploma! Finally one day the State Employment Office sent me for an interview with a company which needed someone with my skills. Here I found a woman owned the shop. She showed me around but I soon got the impression that she was looking for a man and not a worker. I was scared. I thought maybe this was some kind of trap and I would get into trouble again. She said she would let me know about the job later. I never heard from her. Maybe I was too cold.

I was constantly encouraged by Tony Sorrentino and the other members of the West Side Community Committee and finally they helped me get a job in my trade. I worked on this job for over 10 years and built up a good record. In later years I worked in construction and learned another trade.

But I realized that this West Side Community Committee, which had sprouted while I was in prison, was something that I could lean on. Looking back now, I am more aware of what it was doing. At the time I merely sensed that this was a place where I was welcome and where I could go for help. And I sure felt good when they asked me to be a member of the organization —a director! There were three other guys in the Committee too who had the same background, but this was no problem to no one. We were all together, fellows of our neighborhood who had a good time when we got together and at the same time did something good for our neighborhood.

Like the others, I did my little bit of work at our summer camp which we built and I sure got a big kick out of this work. As a member, I helped in other ways. I would do my share when we ran dances or carnivals to raise money for our program. I would volunteer my time working at the carnivals or go out to ask businessmen for donations. One of the interesting things we did was to go to the State Training School for Boys to visit young fellows from our neighborhood. Having been on that side of the fence, I realized what this meant and was only too glad to visit these boys, talk to them, and make them feel we wanted to help them.

I have been tied up with the WSCC now for almost 25 years, very seldom missing a meeting or any of the affairs. I keep a membership card with me all the time so when I get stopped by the cops—yes, still!—I can just flash my card and say, "Why, I belong to this organization. We send kids to camp and prevent juvenile delinquency," (laughing to myself) and the cops look at me kind of suspicious like and off they go.

As I said before, when I came out of prison everything was strange and I didn't know what I was going to do or how things were to turn out for me. Looking back now, if I had fallen in with a different bunch I might have gone into some racket. But instead I fell in with fellows who had a different outlook and a darn good idea, so naturally I got into these different community activities. But now there is no doubt of my future. My life is set. I am married, have children and have a regular job. And as long as I live I will always do my share of community work.

I've been asked, "What effect would you say that your prison experience had on you?" The effect is a thing you carry with you for the rest of your life. You get sent to prison, you serve your sentence, and pay your debt to society, but then you come out a marked man for the rest of your life. The odds are nine to one against you. After all a guy does have a right to make a living. What do they expect a guy to do? He gets convicted, serves his time, and gets released. But not as a free man with opportunities to start to make a decent living. To tell the truth, I was lucky. The first year was hard, but then after that, things began to look better: I had my family and the Committee. The fellows around the Committee helped change my thinking. If it wasn't for the Committee I would probably have gone back with the others who were on the other side of the law and ended up in prison again. Tony Sorrentino and the other fellows were always trying to get me interested in something and keep my mind occupied. The surroundings at the Committee were different than hanging on the corners: most of the fellows were employed and didn't have their minds on making an easy dollar like the crowd I had known.

Today, all my friends are members of the Committee, we spend a lot of time together, visiting each other's homes and the like. Now and then I meet fellows I knew in prison, but I am never lured to go back to any life of crime because now I can't. I would be letting too many people down who have faith in me.

James

I've been with the West Side Community Committee since the day I got out of prison and they have treated me like a man; my past has never been brought up to me or anything done to offend me. When I come to the Committee office for meetings or to the children's center, as soon as I enter the door, why if there's one person or if there's fifty, everyone of them will shake your hand and ask you how you're feeling, how you're doing, and they really are interested in you. They are not the kind of people that will shake your hand and forget about you; they are really interested in you and your family and want to see you get ahead. They are not the type that if you have something they're jealous of you, in fact, if one has something he's willing to share with others. You just feel at home when you go there at night for meetings or to go and help at the children's center with other volunteers. They are a good group of real nice people and we get to talking about different things and you also get to know and understand the children at the center. I've always liked children. It seems like I just fit into the recreation program at night when I volunteer my time one night a week. I help the Committee not because I owe them anything monetary, but yet I feel I do owe them something. I know I have friends there and when you find friends like I have, I go out of my way to keep them.

As I stated before, I am helping at the recreation center sponsored by the West Side Community Committee and I take my son with me too, since it gives me an opportunity to be with my boy. He enjoys it, and I wanted the members to know that I was helping, not because I was obligated to them, but because I enjoyed it and wish to continue doing so, and this is from my heart, not just to be writing words. I really mean it. Nick Taccio never showed me that I was obligated to him or any member of the Committee, and I'll do all I can to help them or anybody that is in trouble because I've received a lot of help which is appreciated. You feel so much better when you know someone is helping you and behind you.

Since I've been with the Committee I was made a member of the Board of Directors, and being considered a newcomer there, I felt good about it. Of course my wife and family feel the same way. The majority of the members know what I am, what I've been. If they were against me, they would never have nominated me for the Board. I found out later that this fellow, the volunteer member I have been working with at the recreation center, was the one that suggested my name for the Board.

When you attend a meeting of the Committee you find everyone sitting around like a happy family. After the business is done, you have coffee and refreshments, talk over family matters, talk about your job and things like that. It's not like a business club, it's a place where you get together and get to know each other and still have enjoyment. My wife's been to some of the meetings with me, she has gone with my son at times, and she's glad I joined up and will become more active herself.

I know the Committee is doing a lot for youngsters. It makes you feel good to know that there are good people in this world. I've met new people that I've never seen before and they took me and treated me like a brother. Today it's hard to find people like that. At the Committee there's young people, middle aged, and there's the old folks too. They just feel that you are one of them and they want you to feel at home. The majority of these people knew my background, they're accepting me for what I am and not for what I was.

When you get to a place like the Committee, you know what you think of the persons you meet, but you don't know what they're thinking of you and that is constantly in the back of your mind. Until you are relieved of that feeling, you are a little tense. After awhile you get to see that these people really want you to become part of them in the organization and they enjoy your company and everything then you start feeling more at ease. It seems like everytime I go there I'm just that much closer to them.

I've been invited to homes and different places by people that I've met for the first time. They never knew me until I came home and they've extended all kinds of invitations. It makes you feel good to know that they are honest and hard working people, which is the kind of people I want to associate with. I've been invited to their homes and I've invited them to our home and we've got some real nice friendships and I really enjoy this.

When I go somewhere today into places you have known and meet people I've known for years, I have some strange feelings. The first thing a lot of them will ask you is about the prison. I'm trying to forget that place and you can't if people constantly ask you questions about it. I feel inferior or something whenever I talk to these people, but that don't mean that I'm afraid of them or anything; I just don't feel at ease. I just can't express myself the way I should or the way I would like to. This reminds me of my experience when I first came home and my wife and I went downtown to see a movie.

After we left the bus, we had to walk a few blocks to the movie house, I kept turning around and my wife asked me "What's troubling you? You just don't seem natural." I said, "Well, I'll tell you, honey. It seems like everyone is staring at me. It seems like I'm walking around with a sign on my back, I just got out of the penitentiary." My wife said, "It isn't so. You just feel that way. You're just self-conscious. You will get over this." I said, "No, I just get the feeling that they are all watching me," and to show you how bad I did feel, I wouldn't even walk up to the ticket window to purchase the tickets. I let my wife buy the tickets. But now, I don't have to worry about anyone behind me because I'm working and I'm going to stay working and I won't have to look around. I know that every week my check will be coming in and I won't have to worry about the next week.

The job that I am working on at the present time was made available through contacts at the West Side Community Committee. When I left the prison, I had a factory job waiting for me and I worked at this for some time. Since that job, I have had a number of other jobs in factories and I had an idea about trying outside work on construction. I mentioned this to Nick Taccio one time and he said that there was a good possibility of going into this field of work because there were several members of the Committee that were in this work for a number of years. It was about a month later that I attended a Committee meeting and Nick Taccio introduced me to one of the members (Sam DeLeo). He told this fellow that I was interested in getting a job on construction and this fellow said that things were somewhat slack at the present time but that around the spring time they would be needing some new workers. This fellow promised that he would make a job available for me and would keep in touch with Nick Taccio.

It was about two months later when Nick called me at home and said that I could start on the construction job the following week. There were a few things that had to be done before starting this new job; one was to get a union card, and Nick Taccio took me to the union office and arrangements were made. The following day I started on the construction job I've held since that day. Now you take this fellow from the Committee that helped me, I've only seen him twice in my life at the Committee meetings, but he was willing to do this for Nick and myself. How can you help but like people like that? I want to show these people that anything they do for me will be appreciated, and I will not let them down.

The above is a personal presentation of the experience and process of rehabilitation of adult offenders by means of encouraging them to participate in community organizations. This is a sound means of proceeding and is supported by the following statement (Waldron, 1976):

> One of the more significant developments in probation and parole has been the involvement of the community at different levels of the rehabilitative process. Community participation is noticeable in the expansion of the use of nonprofessionals, more commonly known as volunteers. A number of new projects involve volunteer opportunities for individual citizens as well as projects for civic organizations (. . .). More recent innovations involve the indigenous nonprofessional in corrections.

Waldron goes on to quote an article on "indigenous nonprofessionals":

> Most professional corrections workers agree that a large segment of their clientele are, by virtue of their norms, values, and life styles, alienated from the mainstream—middle class professionals . . . The indigenous worker, conversely, has often experienced situations and problems similar to those that beset certain clients.

Chapter 7

PROFILES OF NEIGHBORHOOD
ORGANIZATIONS I

Historical Background

When community or neighborhood committees were organized by the Chicago Area Project in 1934 they represented a radical innovation in the field of delinquency prevention. Critics contended that local residents were not qualified to manage and operate youth welfare programs. The community workers who were indigenous leaders and assigned to organize neighborhood committees were considered "untrained" by the traditional agency executives in the city. For many years, both Clifford Shaw (the founder of the Project) and the entire enterprise were considered unorthodox. However, what started as an experiment in three neighborhoods soon developed into a social movement.

After the first three neighborhoods were organized in areas occupied predominantly by white residents, requests were made by black leaders to launch similar projects in their neighborhoods. Within a decade about 10 neighborhood committees were organized and operating successfully in the south side and west side ghetto areas. Today there are over 30 neighborhood committees operating in Chicago and a similar number of municipal and township committees in suburban areas that embody the principles of the Chicago Area Project.

Neighborhood committees have also been organized in many smaller cities and towns in downstate Illinois. For example, over 20 years ago the Quincy Area Project, based on the Chicago model, was established and five neighborhood committees were developed. They are still operating and thriving as significant self-help programs for the prevention of delinquency.

The Rock Island Area Project was recently organized and neighborhood committees are operating in Rockford, Moline, Peoria, Springfield, East St. Louis, and other downstate communities.

DIFFICULTIES ENCOUNTERED

Many problems are encountered in any delinquency prevention effort. Some of these problems are in the nature of powerful forces operating in low-income communities, in the society at large, and those that are inherent in democratic action programs. The first and more basic set of problems grows out of the fact that the social life of the inner-city areas lacks stability and cohesion. It is characterized by conflict of values and absence of consensus on basic problems. In these low-income areas many of the most common forms of crime readily become established in the traditions of the community in the form of gangs and organized crime. The fact that crime becomes embodied in very powerful criminal and political organizations in such urban areas is too well known to need elaboration here.

One aspect of the life in low-income areas that tends to disrupt the unity of the neighborhood is the diversity of competing groups. Conflict among political parties, factions, national or provincial groups, gangs, religious, ethnic, and racial groups often interferes with collective action. For example, in one community, certain groups have been in such severe competition and conflict that it has not been possible, except for temporary periods, for the residents to establish and develop a neighborhood youth welfare program. Thus, unless there is at least some degree of consensus in a community, concerted action is virtually impossible.

Population changes, urban renewal, new highways, and public housing projects also have in some instances destroyed the old neighborhoods. As a result, the work of local committees suffers and must be reorganized. Furthermore, the growth and expansion of the city and the accelerated mobility of modern life have continued to weaken the neighborhood and the traditional forms of social control. These changes in modern life further complicate efforts to carry on neighborhood welfare work.

Moreover, there are also other reasons why it will be more difficult in the years ahead to develop neighborhood programs and other types of welfare activities in the low-income areas in urban communities. For example, 40 years ago, when the Area Project program was launched, the inner-city areas were inhabited predominantly by European groups who brought with them strong institutions such as family, the church, and governmental agencies. These institutions gave stability during the assimilative process and helped these groups to make the transition from the old world to the new. The newcomers to the city today are migrants from the rural South where isolation, racial barriers, and limited opportunities have worked against the development of strong basic institutions adequate for city life. As a result, the development of neighborhood programs among migrant groups are faced with more serious problems than were their predecessors. In addition, there is reason to believe that in the expanding city more areas of high rates of delinquency will be created.

Added to these factors are forces outside the community

that often work against the application of the self-help principle of the Area Project. Because of limitation of space, only a few of these can be discussed here. The first obstacle is the problem of the source of control. The concentration of leadership and control of welfare work in the hands of persons of higher economic strata has been challenged, in a small way, by the Chicago Area Project. The widespread disposition to regard residents of low-income areas with suspicion and to question their talents and capacities has resulted in some attempts to bring the control of the program of community committees under a central board. Such an arrangement would, of course, negate the basic principles of the Chicago Area Project. Fortunately, the Board of the Chicago Area Project has constantly avoided this traditional administrative pattern.

Another problem common to enterprises operating under democratic principles is the extent of participation in social programs. Without exception, in the neighborhood organizations encouraged and aided by the Area Project, an effort has been made to encourage the widest possible participation. There are instances, however, where this goal has not been reached. In one instance, the organization, although operating for many years, went out of existence because the original leadership was one clique or faction of the community. However, even in this situation, a new committee with a broader base later was established.

Another possible problem is the domination or exploitation of the citizens' organization, either by a small group of ambitious persons or even by an aggressive member of the staff. Although the work may suffer temporarily when this happens, democratic processes set into action by the residents can ordinarily be expected to solve the problem.

Notwithstanding these and many other problems which, no doubt, are found also in other welfare organizations, there is good basis in our experience to believe that one of the most effective ways to help people in local areas is to aid and encourage them to assume every possible responsibility for the administration, control, and operation of the welfare activities in their community. Local communities will, of course, need the services of governmental and voluntary agencies to help solve many of the problems with which they are confronted. But the value of such services can be enhanced, if they are made available, not on a superimposed basis but through an instrumentality of local residents who constitute one of the greatest resources for solving human problems and for building better communities.

What then are the distinctive features of these self-help neighborhood committees? What is the structure, program, and function of these groups? What do such organizations actually accomplish? In an attempt to answer these questions, brief descriptions of selected neighborhood committees will be presented in this and the following chapters. The examples that follow represent a good cross section of the 30 organizations operating in the city of Chicago.

THE NEAR WEST SIDE COMMUNITY COMMITTEE

History

Within the shadow of the Loop just west of the Chicago River is the Near West Side. Jane Addams did her pioneer work in this area, and Al Capone got started here, too. It was in what was then the heart of this district that, legend has it, Mrs. O'Leary's cow kicked over the lantern that started the Great Chicago Fire. During the Roaring Twenties this neighborhood achieved the zenith of its notoriety and was dubbed the "Bloody Twentieth" by newspapers.

The author worked in this neighborhood from 1934 through 1945 as the first community organizer and director. These experiences, together with the 40-year history of this community venture appear in a separate publication (Sorrentino, 1977).

For several decades, until 1950, the Near West Side had one of the highest rates of delinquency in Chicago. The Chicago Area Project launched one of its first three experimental neighborhood programs for the prevention of delinquency in this low-income area in 1934.

Encouraged and assisted by the Area Project, a group of young men organized the Near West Side Community Committee as a self-help autonomous organization of local residents to plan, promote, and carry on a neighborhood program for the prevention of delinquency. Since that time this neighborhood committee has carried on a wide range of youth welfare activities and taken the leadership to improve the physical and social environment of the community.

From the beginning this Committee has worked closely with local churches, schools, indigenous groups, police, courts, and local institutions. Through such collaboration Parent-Teacher Associations were organized in local schools; a health and sanitation campaign was launched (one concrete achievement was the distribution of 4000 garbage containers); facilities at the local park were improved and expanded; communitywide recreation programs were conducted; and a planning board was established. Such efforts to improve the community have been ongoing during the past four decades. As a result, today the Near West Side is an entirely different and greatly improved neighborhood. Many of the slum properties have been torn down, others renovated, and thousands of new apartments have been constructed. The eastern end of the area, east of Halsted and Polk Streets, was cleared by the City of Chicago and in the early 1960s the University of Illinois, Chicago Circle Campus, was built.

Storefront Centers and Recreation

Over the years the Near West Side Community Committee maintained and operated three storefront neighborhood centers, each under the management and leadership of local adults and young people residing near the Centers. These "drop-in centers" were used primarily as social and recreation centers for children and for meeting places and social functions.

In addition to these centers, the Committee has sponsored communitywide indoor and outdoor athletic events and tournaments in conjunction with the local park and other agencies. The Committee has subsidized neighborhood teams, supported scouting, and organized the activities of over 25 social and athletic clubs. In addition, in 1941 the Committee and Our Lady of Pompeii Church sponsored a dance and "Ad Book," raised $4000 and purchased 44 acres of land located 35 miles from the neighborhood and built a summer camp for children.

Most of the construction work on the mess hall, cabins, and other facilities was done by volunteer workers, some of whom were young men on probation and parole. For about 15 years thousands of children engaged in a summer camp experience at Pompeii Camp as did many adults who used the property for picnics and outings on weekends. However, because of population changes, housing redevelopment and urban renewal, the Committee was unable to operate the camp in later years. A solution was found when another Area Project group, the Near Northwest Civic Committee, assumed the leadership and responsibility for maintaining and operating the camp.

Work with Delinquents

From its inception this Committee has concerned itself with the task of helping children, young people, and adults who have gotten into difficulties with the law. This work began in the streets, using local young men, some of whom were former delinquents. These workers established contacts with street corner groups and gangs and redirected them into constructive activities in the neighborhood. In addition, the Committee receives referrals of delinquent children from schools, parents, and law enforcement agencies. Individual counseling is provided to these children and adolescents and every effort made to incorporate them in the activities of the Committee or in other conventional groups in the neighborhood. Over the years the Committee has also been unusually successful in rehabilitating older offenders. Members of the Committee visit adult offenders while they are in the institutions, work with their families, secure employment, and when the offenders are released they are welcome to join the Committee or participate in some of its activities.

The Committee Today

After 40 years, the community work initiated by the Area Project in 1934 is being continued by the Near West Side Community Committee. Two other Committees that started at the same time disbanded about 15 years ago because of population changes and organizational problems. It is remarkable, therefore, that this organization is still functioning, although there have been many difficulties, problems, and social changes: loss of population; urban renewal and the demolition of about one-third of the area for the University of Illinois, Circle Campus; leadership problems; and personality conflicts.

The Committee operates today from a storefront center at 624 S. Racine Avenue and continues to plan and promote a wide variety of youth welfare programs in conjunction with many public and private agencies. It has a budget of approximately $27,000, of which $4300 is allocated by the Chicago Area Project.

BEATRICE CAFFREY YOUTH SERVICE

Overcrowding, economic deprivation and inequalities, discrimination, conflicting systems of moral values, and social disorganization have contributed to the higher rates of delinquency on Chicago's South Side as compared with other areas in and around Chicago. The mass of human breakdown and the wreckage that mounts up here in a narrow strip of land only 7 miles long and 4½ miles wide, crammed with over a half million people, hardly seems to be the place to undertake a self-help community action program. Yet here is where several groups of local residents, aided by the Area Project and state workers, undertook a grass-roots organization that involves the active participation of local residents and the cooperation of indigenous institutions.

The Beatrice Caffrey Youth Service (BCYS) was organized in the Grand Boulevard area in 1950 under the leadership of Mrs. Sadie Jones. It was started by a group of women who volunteered their services to the Junvenile Court and furnished "Big Sisters" for black delinquent girls. Known as the Women's City-Wide Committee, it was reorganized and incorporated as the Beatrice Caffrey Youth Service, named after one of its dedicated volunteers who had passed away. After operating out of rented space on Michigan Avenue and 50th Street for several years, the group decided to purchase an old building at 213 E. 50th Place. Now fully paid for and renovated, this three-story building serves as the headquarters, office, and community center where a varied program for children, adolescents, and adults takes place. Activities include recreation and sports, music instruction, bands, tutoring, crafts, group work, tours, counseling, and social action projects to improve health, housing, employment, and race relations.

Problem children are referred for assistance by schools, police, courts, other agencies, and families. The BCYS provides counseling for the child and family, invites them to participate in its various activities, intervenes on their behalf with official agencies in attempting to work out satisfactory plans for treatment, and often provides financial assistance, employment, or referral to other resources. In addition, the BCYS sponsors many communitywide events of a social, cultural, or educational nature. For example, the annual Lincoln Day Conference involves over 500 adults and young people in discussion of youth and community problems and recognizes outstanding volunteers. The Annual Merit Dinner attracts as many as 1000 persons to honor one or more distinguished leaders in the black community, while the annual Blue Ribbon Tea on a Sunday afternoon is attended by several thousand persons who contribute over $12,000 yearly.

While the BCYS is structured somewhat differently from the other Area Project committees, it operates on the same principles and philosophy. It has a board of directors similar to the other committees; however, its program is carried on with and through six other neighborhood committees, each with its own volunteers. These volunteers hold meetings in homes, churches, housing projects, and sponsor civic and educational projects in cooperation with schools, urban progress centers, and, of course, with the Commission on Delinquency Prevention, a group that furnishes a staff of six community workers under the direction of E. Toy Fletcher.

Another special project that grew out of the interests of Mrs. Jones and her volunteers was Half-Way House, built in Crestwood, Illinois. Designed to provide residential care for girls judged to be in need of supervision by the Juvenile Court, this new building, named the Sadie Waterford Manor, constructed at a cost of $350,000, accommodates 14 girls. It has taken these citizens from disadvantaged areas over 20 years to raise the money for this project. Dedicated volunteers are the instruments for the success of these programs, but the chief driving force has been Mrs. Jones, who though 89 years young, continues to give dynamic leadership to this enterprise.

Near Northwest Civic Committee

Chicago's Near Northwest Side is an area of light manufacturing plants, commercial enterprises, and small business establishments interspersed with residential sections. It is bounded on the north by a wide stretch of railroad tracks and coal yards. To the south, close by, is West Madison Street, a notorious honky tonk and flophouse strip. For many years the Near Northwest Side was one of the three areas of Chicago from which the Boys' Court drew most of its cases. High rates of infant mortality, tuberculosis, and relief cases prevailed here too. Each group of people, regardless of national extraction, experienced these problems while they lived in the area. As these earlier groups improved their economic circumstances they moved out, but they left behind the bulk of their social ills to be perpetuated by those who remained.

Although the people of the Near Northwest Side were cognizant of this and wished to alter their pattern of life, they found it difficult to begin. It was not until their neighbors heard about the Chicago Area Project that Near Northwest Siders learned how they might alleviate these social problems. As they heard more and more about what was being accomplished in other areas, those of the Near Northwest Side decided to organize in similar fashion. In 1941, with the assistance of the Chicago Area Project, a small group of residents banded together and incorporated themselves as the Near Northwest Civic Committee. They rented a large storefront and launched a recreational program, scouting, street work with corner groups, and of course, with delinquents and delinquent gangs. Over the years the area has changed from a predominantly Italian neighborhood to a mixture of many other ethnic groups which, in addition to Italians includes Poles, Puerto Ricans, and native whites, all actively involved in the work of this committee.

The Committee's Center, at 1329 West Grand Avenue, is the scene of many community activities. Committee meetings and many social functions are held there, and it is in constant use by children, teenage groups, and Boy Scout troops under the sponsorship of the Committee and local volunteers. At Christmastime, parties are given at the Center for over 2000 youngsters. Besides its recreation program, this Center under the leadership of Thomas Brindisi and Frank Butero provides counseling to children and families who are confronted with problems. The Committee also has conducted classes in citizenship training and have intervened on behalf of local youth or adults in resolving problems with the police, courts, health department, Veterans Administration, and other social agencies. A few years ago the Committee carried on a special campaign to improve housing and sponsored a conservation and rehabilitation program. Buildings in dangerous condition were repaired or torn down, and many buildings were completely remodeled both inside and out. As already mentioned, this Committee today operates Pompeii Camp, described earlier.

Local businesspeople in this area are actively involved in the work of this Committee, more than they are in the other Area Project units. They generously support the program and some serve on the board of directors. There are many reasons why these businesspeople and local residents feel at home here: it is because Dan Brindisi, like all generous persons, undertakes a mission with a spirit of old-time hospitality that includes good wine, and enormous amounts of food. When people "break bread" in this enjoyable manner "esprit de corps" exists, and people are highly motivated to help the organization achieve its objective.

HEGEWISCH COMMUNITY COMMITTEE

The Hegewisch community, located on Chicago's southeastern tip, where Lake Michigan rounds the bend into Indiana, is the gateway to America's inland empire of steel. A profusion of smokestacks and grain elevators rise against the sky. Auto and steel plants surround it. Ships laden with raw materials have come to Hegewisch from all over the world. From Hegewisch to all the world have gone implements of war and peace. But there is more to Hegewisch than meets the eye. Beneath this monument to industrial engineering is a story of social engineering, a story of men and women and changes they brought about in their community.

The story begins in 1940 when several residents became concerned about an increasing rate of juvenile delinquency. They realized the problem could not be solved simply by arresting offenders. Besides, the children probably were not always to blame. It was usually a case of their coming into contact with conditions to be found in any highly industrialized community. In addition to other factors, delinquency was indeed a product of environment. The answer, it seemed to the residents, could be found only by starting where the problem started.

They began with a small recreational program in an abandoned store building which they remodeled. They joined forces with the local park, churches, schools, police, and service clubs —pooling both the human and institutional resources—and established the Hegewisch Community Committee as a clearinghouse for virtually every phase of community activity and welfare.

The Committee office and headquarters today, located at 13248 Baltimore, under the leadership of Ann Hamilton, executive director, serves as the only youth and community welfare organization in this multiethnic community of approximately 20,000 people.

The Hegewisch Community Committee sponsors communitywide social, recreational, and educational programs, a unique tutoring program, "Reading and 'Riding,' " combining remedial reading and educational tours all under the leadership of volunteers; individual counseling and treatment services for delinquents, drug users, and individuals confronted with other problems; and information and referral services on health, employment, and public assistance programs. By keeping open lines of communication with residents, community leaders, and institutions, the Committee enables the community to be constantly aware of the needs and problems of the people and maintains an enterprise that can furnish appropriate social action in an effort to deal with all problems and issues.

Finally, even more convincingly for Hegewisch than for the other committees operating in disrupted areas, the work done by the Hegewisch Committee has been instrumental in reducing the rate of delinquency and number of commitments to correctional institutions by an appreciable amount.

MEXICAN COMMUNITY COMMITTEE OF SOUTH CHICAGO

In South Chicago, around the sprawling steel mills, is a small neighborhood occupied largely by about 15,000 persons of Mexican extraction. It has existed as an isolated ethnic community for over 40 years, since its people did not feel a need in the early days of immigration to embrace American culture. Life here revolved around the church, the mills, and the omnipresent taverns that were as much banks and clubhouses as drinking places. Like other immigrant groups, the Mexicans were faced with problems of acculturation and acceptance in a world dominated by "Anglos." Their language problems, cultural background, and limited occupational skills set them apart and made difficult their active participation in the wider community. This social situation, coupled with poor housing and meager economic resources, were some of the factors that resulted in delinquency and other social problems.

Gradually, however, as the second generation became Americanized through the schools, churches, and places of employment, the Mexican people began to participate in community affairs, developed their own social groups, and began to exercise leadership in both indigenous and nonindigenous institutions.

In 1959 the social climate seemed favorable for the organization and development of a community organization. A group of Mexican leaders who knew about the work of the Russell Square Community Committee in the "Polish Bush" area adjoining the Mexican neighborhood, called upon the Chicago Area Project to assist them in establishing a similar enterprise. Henry Martinez, a local resident, was employed by the state, and the Chicago Area Project provided seed money to help organize the Mexican Community Committee of South Chicago (MCC).

Now in its eighteenth year, this committee attempts to carry on programs that meet the needs of residents of all ages. The Committee cooperates in this endeavor by cooperating with churches, schools, parks, settlement houses, and other private and public agencies. Last year the Committee purchased its own four-story building that serves as the focal point for the many recreational and athletic events sponsored throughout the year. An especially significant part of the committee's program is its collaboration with the schools. Priority is given to the task of assisting Mexican children in overcoming language handicaps by bridging the gap between the school and the home. Lines of communication are maintained with all schools, problems are identified, and joint projects are undertaken. At its annual dinner meeting, the committee presents Educator Awards to those principals and teachers who have made an outstanding contribution to community service.

Like all other community committees, the MCC works diligently with police and court officials to assist young people who get into trouble. These agencies often seek the assistance of this organization in formulating plans to reincorporate the delinquent into the constructive life of the community.

LAWNDALE COMMUNITY COMMITTEE

Before 1950 Lawndale was a fashionable, middle-class community with a predominantly Jewish population of approximately 100,000. It was a strong, stable community with excellent apartment buildings and houses, lawns, trees, and many synagogues, community centers, and educational institutions that adequately met the needs of its residents. This community was the setting for Meyer Levin's novel, *The Old Bunch.* During and after World War II the Jewish families started to move to Skokie and other suburbs. With the housing shortage, many of the two- and three-story buildings were being illegally converted and black migrants from the South started to move in. Within 10 years the population in this area almost doubled without any new housing being constructed. A two-flat building in which two families lived now began to house four or five families.

Just as the population changes started, congestion and deterioration set in, the morale of the residents was low, and the behavior of the adolescents began to get out of hand. In this unstable situation emerged a rather large group of Jewish, Irish, and Italian teenagers. Most were out of school, out of work, and not in military service. Detached and alienated from the conventional institutions and agencies, they resorted to drugs, drinking, delinquency, and violent behavior. Most of the members of this group had official records of delinquency and some had served time in institutions for offenders. These groups engaged in a great deal of vandalism, destroying property of local schools, social agencies, and even business establishments. Many of the boys carried weapons and used them in armed robberies or in fights with rival gangs.

One day, a meeting of agency leaders was called to discuss what might be done to cope with the depredations of this gang, to try to reach them and offer to redirect them. Some of the agency workers admitted their inability to deal with them. It was reported that on one occasion the boys were invited to a community center for an event and it ended up with the boys starting fights and causing serious damage. The agency people were about to give up when the principal of a special school suggested they discuss this problem with Clifford Shaw. Shaw agreed to help by providing one of our community workers, Joseph Loscuito, selected because of his unique background and experience.

For establishing rapport with tough delinquent gangs, Joe Loscuito is one of the most capable street workers. He has no academic degrees, but he is streetwise. His training, like so many of our good workers, was secured by experience. Loscuito grew up on the Near North Side, described by Harvey Warren Zorbaugh in *The Gold Coast and the Slum,* in the vicinity of "death corner," the Sicilian ghetto now occupied by Cabrini-Green Homes, a housing project with a row of 19-story structures, dubbed by the press and sociologists as high-rise slums, and a black ghetto.

Loscuito began by contacting the Lawndale gang boys in their hangouts along Roosevelt Road, on the streets, poolrooms, and snack shops. He was not suspect because he had the traits of a street-corner boy himself. Besides, there is nothing formidable or overbearing about him. A small man with thick glasses and high forehead, he does not present a threatening image. Actually, any of the boys could easily have overpowered him. But Loscuito had no fear or at least showed none. He had grown up with similar boys and men who were in the rackets and therefore had no difficulty relating to the boys, and they began to trust and confide in him. He was thus able to help individual boys with school or family problems and intervene on their behalf with police and court officials. These efforts naturally brought him in contact with parents and other adults. In his discussion Loscuito discovered that while the parents were disturbed and bewildered, they were willing to participate in a community effort to develop a program to deal with the gang, and above all to prevent the younger boys from following in the footsteps of the older adolescents currently caught in the web of the juvenile justice system.

After a few months Joe Loscuito detected that there was sufficient interest among the adults to organize a community committee. A group of about 50 adults started to meet in the basement apartment of one of the members and discussed plans to develop a program. The group formally organized in 1949 as the Lawndale Community Committee and received its charter in 1950 as a nonprofit corporation. By this time, however, persons active in this committee started to move further north in the vicinity of Roosevelt Road and Pulaski. The leaders discovered that the nearby Fillmore Police Station had available an entire floor above the station that had been unused for years. The Committee negotiated with the City of Chicago and made arrangements to have free use of this space as its head-quarters and as a youth and community center.

Admittedly there were some drawbacks in operating a center actually on top of the police station. It was feared that the delinquents would not come in and that the community would generally be cool to the idea. However, the leaders in the community committee began to talk to their neighbors and interpreted their plans and goals. When the Center was dedicated it was very well attended and further help was pledged. The Center soon became a successful operation and provided game rooms, craft shops, pool tables, club rooms, and facilities for boxing and various social and educational activities.

The Lawndale Community Committee continues to oper-ate to this date, but there have been changes, both in the compo-sition of the membership and in the community. As the white residents moved away from the neighborhood, the committee leaders invited and encouraged the participation of black resi-dents. As a result, the membership today is predominantly black. To facilitate this changeover, the Area Project in 1959 assigned John Harris to be the community worker to assist the Committee. A few years prior to this assignment John Harris had been in the area maintaining liaison with the street gangs, local agencies, and the Institute for Juvenile Research. This was during the peak of gang activity in Lawndale. The Vice Lords, the Egyptian Cobras, the Imperial Chaplains, the King Clovers and other tough street gangs were very prominent in the area, claiming the loyalty and participation of thousands of young people.

Following Harris' initial contacts with these groups, the Chicago Youth Centers, which had been organized a few years prior under the leadership of Elliott Donnelley, a member of the Area Project Board, started to assign "detached workers" to work with gangs. In time these efforts redirected the energies of these gangs into conventional channels. Together with other healing and stabilizing influences at work in the community, the incidence of violence and delinquency over the past 10 years has been substantially reduced.

With John Harris assuming responsibility for assisting the Lawndale Community Committee in 1959, Joe Loscuito was transferred to the North Side where he organized and developed the Mid-North Community Committee. Its structure and program is comparable to the other community committees already described.

When John Harris retired several years ago, Lavergne Luster was assigned as the community worker by the Commission on Delinquency Prevention.

The space in the police station that served as the Committee's Center was torn down a few years ago and today operates out of a storefront facility.

Chapter 8

PROFILES OF NEIGHBORHOOD
ORGANIZATIONS II

SOUTH CHICAGO ORGANIZED FOR PEOPLE'S EFFORTS

They said Millgate could not be organized. They said Millgate residents were complacent with their lot and refused to be stirred from the community's "self-imposed isolation." But they were wrong.

One day several years ago at the South Chicago YMCA, something happened that was not supposed to happen. Sixteen people met that day. Three—Anthony Sorrentino, Mrs. Sadie Jones, and Joanne Mitchell—were from the Community Services Juvenile Division of the Illinois Department of Corrections. They had come to sell a plan for community organization and 13 were community people who bought it. In 1976, these state services were transferred to the newly created Illinois Commission on Delinquency Prevention. The timing could not have been better. The community leaders had seen changes in their area and were concerned. Myriad problems were facing them: poor housing, shaky educational institutions, a political system that was unresponsive to their needs, and a lack of services and facilities that were trapping their children in a vicious quagmire of juvenile delinquency. Fortunately they were not novices because they had made prior attempts to organize. Some present represented three generations of a family that had been active in community work in Millgate.

This time, however, there was something different. Staff from the Illinois Department of Corrections and the prospect of seed money from the Chicago Area Project put them further ahead of the game than previous groups had been. Trained staff and seed money were the catalysts to coalesce this group.

At the conclusion of the 4-hour meeting, officers had been elected, eight working committees had been designated, $35 was donated toward a treasury, and South Chicago Organized for People's Efforts (SCOPE) was born.

Millgate was stirring.

In order to appreciate the significance of an organization such as SCOPE coming into being, one has to know something of the Millgate area.

Millgate derives its name from the fact that it begins where the gates of the steel mills end. It is the oldest section of the South Chicago community which, itself, has a history older than the present City of Chicago. Millgate is bounded by 87th Street on the north, 92nd Street on the south, and the Illinois Central tracks on the west. Because of its territorial boundaries and many other factors, the neighborhood seems to be isolated physically from the rest of the city, and some old-timers say it is ignored politically.

1. There are 6200 people in Millgate. Ninety-two percent are black-American, 4 percent are Mexican-American, and 3 percent are white.
2. Four thousand three hundred residents are under the age of 18.
3. The average family has eight children; this is significant because recreational facilities in the area include one tot lot, one ballfield, and a wading pool.

4. The median income is $3150.
5. Seventy-seven percent of the families are related to public assistance, and 56 percent of the heads of household are on public aid.
6. Of the population over 18, 21.6 percent are unemployed, accounting for the second-highest unemployment rate in the nation, surpassed only by Seattle, Washington.
7. Eighteen percent are underemployed, and only 5 percent reach an acceptable financial level deemed to be within the mainstream of American society.

Housing has always been a problem in Millgate. Currently:

1. Thirty-five percent of the available housing units are unfit for human habitation and, although pending condemnation by the courts, are still inhabited.
2. Forty-one percent of the housing units have multiple violations (over 15).
3. Fifteen percent have other minor violations.
4. Nine percent of the units are vacant.

Source for this social data on Millgate comes from the 1966 Community Survey made by the Illinois State Employment Service.

There has been great mobility away from the community. There is no mobility inward. This is partly due to the substandard housing in existence, plus the Urban Renewal decision to redevelop the area, which has created apathy on the part of homeowners and landlords, resulting in building violations that endanger life and health and allowing deterioration to a great degree. Although there are a few homes within the area that are still maintaining themselves, vandalism, destruction of housing units by fire, or demolition because of vacancy has decreased the units tremendously within recent years. Some housing units have been lost, and rightfully so, but there have been no replacements. The first new construction in this area *since the 1800s* were a number of private homes on 89th and Mackinaw. Since that time there have been two apartment units built—one having 15 units, the other 25. These were built in the early 1960s and there has been little construction since.

Reverend Osborne said, when he first came to South Chicago in the 1960s, that there were people still burning coal stoves. The average home in the area now is still not centrally heated. Some of the residents have said, only half-jokingly, their housing is in such poor condition that in the winter they have to dress up to go to bed.

Millgate is devastated; rodent control is a problem, lead poisoning is prevalent, and all symptoms bred by poor housing are present. In addition, there are no health facilities, no doctors, no dentists, and no lawyers.

According to the Public Information Office of the Chicago Police Department, the community is located within a police district experiencing an upsurge in crime. Millgate ranks as an area of high rate of juvenile delinquency.

From 1965 to 1970, the Illinois Department of Corrections has had committed to it 38 boys and 7 girls from the Millgate area. There is a lack of economic development in the community witnessed by the fact that there are only 17 business houses existing, 4 of which are owned by local residents.

When SCOPE was organized in 1969, a militant faction, whose rhetoric preached that black Americans cannot have their needs fulfilled by working within the American system, had been attempting to gain a foothold in Millgate; they found believers. SCOPE attempted to provide alternatives and to show that grievances can be redressed and needs fulfilled by working within the system. During the past 10 years SCOPE has demonstrated that progress can be made to cope with some of the problems with which residents are confronted through a self-help neighborhood organization.

Getting Started

During its first few months SCOPE held weekly meetings at the South Chicago YMCA to organize its structure, recruit volunteers, and formulate plans for a youth program and neighborhood improvement projects. With a grant of $500 from the Chicago Area Project, matched by SCOPE, a bank account was started. Fundraising events included a bake sale, a sidewalk sale, sale of dinners, and individual contributions. These fundraising events have continued over the years and today this organization raises approximately $5000 annually, an amount matched with Community Fund money allocated through the Chicago Area Project.

Recreational Activities

SCOPE provides a varied sports and recreational program in its storefront center and utilizes other space in empty lots and churches for such activities as the Blue Berets Drill Team; Pom-Pom, a girls' marching group; basketball and softball teams; and Afro-American and modern dancing classes. Other activities include classes on tutoring, hygiene and charm, and home economics.

Cooperating with Local Agencies

SCOPE members recognized the importance of working with the agencies and institutions in the South Chicago community. Accordingly, they established liaison with the political organizations, churches, schools, and social welfare agencies in hopes that such institutions would make available new resources for the residents of Millgate. These included needed services and facilities for mental health, legal services, emergency aid, special education classes for underachievers, housing, and urban renewal.

For the past several years the City's Department of Human Services has provided a part-time youth worker, several

CETA workers (through the federally funded Comprehensive Employment and Training Act) and subsidizes the day-care program.

As a result of these efforts many new services and programs have been made available. As one resident said, "The days of the mythical self-imposed isolation are over for Millgate."

There is still much to be done in Millgate, but the important thing is that the residents and leaders have organized, are carrying on many constructive programs, and have accepted the challenge to work toward the improvement of their neighborhood.

THE TRUMBULL PARK COMMUNITY COMMITTEE

History

This Committee is based in the Trumbull Park Homes, a public housing project, located in South Deering. There are 447 row-house units with a population of 1445. The total population of the neighborhood, however, is 4395, of which 2037 are of Spanish descent, and 175 are blacks.

For years, staff members of the state's Community Services Unit had rendered services to juveniles living in this area and had suggested to leaders that they organize into a neighborhood committee. Some of these volunteers became acquainted with the work of the Hegewisch Community Committee and the Mexican Community Committee in 1969 and, after several meetings, formally became a committee chartered as a nonprofit corporation in July 1970.

The public housing management was familiar with the valuable efforts of the other neighborhood committees and gave full support to the Trumbull Park Community Committee (TPCC). Space consisting of a large room, 30 by 45 feet, plus two small rooms was assigned for full use free.

From its beginning, the Committee faced the major challenge of persuading residents outside of the Project to join and work together.

Crafts are taught twice a week, 4 hours each day. Sewing classes are held once a week, as are meetings of the Junior Science Club. The committee supports various scholarship programs. Eight local high school graduates (mostly Latins and blacks) are attending Mt. Senario College in Ladysmith, Wisconsin, on scholarships and work-study sponsored by the committee.

Since drug abuse is a major problem in Trumbull Park, the Committee is promoting drug abuse education through a local leader who was an addict.

The Committee also leases nearby land for use by its Garden Club, which has 14 plots, all producing vegetables.

Recreation Programs

The Committee supports five Little League teams, two Pony League teams, two boys' basketball teams, one girls' softball, and one girls' volleyball teams. TPCC has also sponsored a very successful boxing show. A daycamp for 100 children is conducted in July and August. Also during the summer the committee operates playground programs for the children.

The committee has a large collection of trophies and other awards on display. The various sports programs generate the most support in the form of volunteer leaders and financial contributions.

Social Services

The Committee also assists families to receive appropriate services from the various welfare systems. For example, the Committee has arranged for various health programs including inoculations and blood tests.

The Committee's pantry is valuable, especially in emergencies when families have no funds for food. One-day-old bread is distributed weekly to 150 families in a program operated by a senior citizen 76 years old.

For each of the past 2 years the committee has spent about $250 to buy shoes for needy children.

Several members of the Committee work closely with the community worker in counseling juveniles referred by the Youth Division of the Police Department and the Juvenile Court. By this assistance many children are diverted from correctional institutions.

Community Involvement

The Committee is very active with many local organizations, it is recognized as an important body, and its cooperation is sought by a variety of groups. It has excellent relationships with the schools, churches, parks, and city service bureaus. Its chairman is one of the most influential members of the Advisory Board of the South Chicago Urban Progress Center. The committee's annual budget is approximately $13,800, of which it raises $10,300, and receives Community Fund allotments of $3500 through the Chicago Area Project.

BIG BUDDIES YOUTH SERVICES

The Big Buddies Youth Services, a group of local citizens in a black ghetto neighborhood on Chicago's South Side, has been unusually successful in rehabilitating delinquents and youthful offenders. "Big Buddies," men and women who grew up in the community and who themselves were the products of deprivation, overcrowded conditions, and limited opportunities, were recruited in 1950 by Alexander H. McDade, a community worker with the State of Illinois and Chicago Area Project.

Some of the key leaders in this group had benefited from their participation in the program of another community committee; hence when Alexander McDade alerted them to the ever-present problems of young people in the Woodlawn and Grand Crossing area who were being processed into the criminal justice system, they responded to his invitation to organize a neighborhood committee whose primary purpose would be to work on an individual basis with problem boys and girls referred by the schools, police, and other law enforcement agencies.

The role of a Buddy is to establish and maintain a significant relationship with one young person who has been in difficulty. The men and women selected for this volunteer work have a genuine interest in youth and possess sensitivity and warmth to enable them to influence the youth with whom he or she is assigned. Buddies make frequent visits to the youth's home and accompany the youth to church, socials, sporting events, and to cultural and educational institutions. In addition, those volunteers have conferences with school principals, teachers, attendance officers, counselors, police, and parole officers to share information and work with them on a mutual basis in attempts to assist the youth in making satisfactory adjustments.

As this work with delinquents was going on, the Buddies met regularly to formulate plans for a broader neighborhood program for the prevention of delinquency. They started to raise funds through various benefit drives and were soon able to rent facilities on the second floor of an old factory. After much renovation this facility became the headquarters for the organization and the recreation center for hundreds of boys and girls.

By 1970, the organization had outgrown its rented facilities and purchased a two-story building at 7145 S. Chicago Avenue. Members of the board provided the down payment and the balance was raised by benefit drives and grants from foundations. One of the fundraising highlights was a benefit performance by Sammy Davis, Jr. at the Mill Run Playhouse.

The new center today enables the Big Buddies Youth Services to carry on a more comprehensive recreation program including a day center. Other facets of the program include educational tours for thousands of children every year.

Westside Youth Boosters and Civic Committee

About 30 years ago East Garfield Park was a middle-class area with a predominantly white population and a relatively low rate of delinquency. With population movement, mobility, and disruption, housing became deteriorated and, by 1960, the area took on the characteristics of a ghetto area with high rates of delinquency.

In 1959, a small group of parents and other interested adults in this community became concerned about the number of children who were becoming delinquent. They observed that the youth officers, often having no alternatives, referred such children to the Juvenile Court. Since these children came from a disrupted community with meager resources, the court often had no alternative but to commit many of the children to correctional institutions.

Residents in the East Garfield neighborhood had heard about the work of community committees in other parts of the city and requested the assistance of the Illinois Youth Commission to organize a similar program in their area. Mrs. Rosetta Wheatfall, an experienced community organizer, was assigned to the area and started to work with local leaders to survey the neighborhood, identify the problems, and formulate strategies for organizing a neighborhood committee and to develop resources needed to launch a program.

After a series of meetings the group decided to call itself the Westside Youth Boosters and Civic Committee (WSYBCC). At first the Committee met in local churches and schools. Here, local residents were invited to meetings and public forums, creating interest, awareness, and consensus on local issues. From the beginning the Committee recognized that the local schools constituted one of the most important resources for the education and socialization of its young people. Instead of attacking the schools for some of their deficiencies, the Committee instead worked closely with the district superintendent and with the principals and teachers on common problems. In the spring of 1960, the committee launched its first annual VIP Banquet (Very Important Persons) honoring at this occasion principals and teachers who supported the committee's program, who displayed special sensitivity toward youth problems, and who contributed their time and talents in helping children with problems.

As the Committee demonstrated ability to raise funds, they were matched by the Chicago Area Project. This enabled them to rent and furnish a three-and-a-half-room suite in a local office building and to launch other projects. Local merchants furnished jobs for young people and the National Youth Corps (NYC) provided young workers who tutored and counseled school children under the supervision of public school teachers. Educational literature was widely distributed to alert parents and children on the danger of lead poisoning and to acquaint them with resources for health services.

Providing leisure time activities has been high on the Committee's list of priorities since it was organized. It has secured the use of the Madison Street Armory for physical fitness training, basketball, and space for scouting, clubs, and other meetings. During the summer, baseball teams are organized and tournaments are sponsored cooperatively with local schools.

The Committee accepts referrals of problem children from parents, schools, and youth officers, and tutoring is provided for these children by trained volunteers and staff members. An essential part of the treatment consists of providing opportunities for these children to participate in the Committee's social and recreational programs and in other conventional activities in the community.

The Westside Youth Boosters and Civic Committee today operates from a storefront center at 17 S. Kedzie under the direction of Alonzo Scott. Its annual budget is aproximately $8000, half of which is provided by the Chicago Area Project. The Commission on Delinquency Prevention assigns a community worker to this committee, and in addition, the City's Department of Human Resources provides a full-time worker. During the summer months approximately 30 CETA workers, funded by the federal government, are assigned. These young workers supervise children in activities at the center, in local playgrounds, and on many trips and outings to parks, museums, and other places of cultural and educational interest.

Without question, the WSYBCC is a valuable human resource that meets the needs of hundreds of children in this low-income area. Moreover, it provides needed personal contact for children when they become involved in difficulties with the law. Unless such intervention takes place, many children are likely to be processed by the impersonal criminal justice system and become further alienated from the conventional life of the community.

MID-NORTH COMMUNITY COMMITTEE

About 20 years ago a semistable neighborhood located in the Lincoln Park area suffered at the hands of 40 boys called "The Earth Angels." They ranged from 14 to 20 years of age and their activities did not in the least complement their name. The closest thing to a "halo" ever worn by these angels was a Chicago "litter" basket dropped on their heads during a fight.

People could not drive their cars through the neighborhood when these boys decided to tie up traffic with their own cars. If some brave soul decided to say something it would result in property damage. If there was a newcomer in the neighborhood this would surely mean a fight and when they started drinking and standing around a street corner, again you could count on fights and more property damage.

This activity showed the residents that the programs conducted by the existing agencies could not meet the challenge of these boys, nor hold their interest.

Fortunately, there was a group of young men residing in this area who were concerned with these problems. They themselves had similar gang experiences and they received guidance and help from a community committee in their former neighborhood. Hence, they realized the value of forming a committee to help solve this neighborhood problem, and most of all, to guide and help these boys.

There were 10 young men in this group. They held informal meetings in local coffee shops and homes to discuss the seriousness of this problem and decided to contact the Illinois Youth Commission's Division of Community Services for help.

After many informal meetings and assistance from Joseph Loscuito, the state community worker, this group of young men decided to form a community committee, elect officers, obtain a state charter, and establish an office and headquarters—and so was born the Mid-North Community Committee (MNCC).

This Committee operates in a neighborhood of working-class people bounded by Armitage and Fullerton Avenues and Halstead and Racine Streets. The buildings, while old, are in fairly good condition and the community, in general, has a neat residential appearance.

The number of children brought to the attention of the local juvenile officers had been increasing each year. In 1959, over 300 juvenile cases were brought to the attention of the local police station, and over 60 delinquent petitions were filed at the Juvenile Court. The offenses ranged from larceny to burglary and gang fights.

In addition to this problem with juveniles, a number of boys over the juvenile age were brought to the attention of the Boys' Court. In 1960, the Committee worked with 20 Boys' Court cases; however, this figure does not tell the whole story and does not include the unofficial cases.

One of the Committee's first problems was that of the Trebes Fieldhouse, operated by the Chicago Park District.

Some segments of the community wanted the Fieldhouse demolished because it was old and it looked bad next to a new half-million dollar school building. The Committee opposed this action and felt that regardless of the age of the building, it served a very good purpose and met the needs of many youngsters. Therefore, several community meetings were held and the Mid-North Community Committee expressed its desire to fight attempts to demolish Trebes Fieldhouse.

The Committee held the firm opinion that the Fieldhouse was an important and necessary resource for leisure time and that with adequate repairs and staff furnished by the Park District it could again become a useful youth center. Accordingly, the Mid-North Community Committee embarked upon a campaign to achieve this goal. The Committee informed the local press and received its support. Political groups, veterans' organizations, and the residents in general were enlisted to support this move.

Finally, after many efforts along this line, the Committee was notified by the Chicago Park District that they would make necessary repairs and make available additional staff to operate this youth center.

A few years later part of the park land was needed for the Oscar Mayer School, and, while Trebes Fieldhouse was torn down, the officials assured the Committee that a playground with outdoor equipment would be provided.

The Committee operated from a storefront center for about 5 years and in 1965 decided to purchase an old two-story building at 1109 West Webster Street. After extensive renovation, with substantial funds contributed by Joseph Mangini, the Committee president, the Center became known as the Mangini Youth Center. This facility provides space for game rooms, club meetings, crafts, counseling, tutoring, parties, and many other social and recreational activities.

When a boy or girl from this neighborhood is apprehended by the local police, members of the Committee intervene on behalf of the youngster. Quite often the local juvenile officer will release these youngsters with the understanding that they work with the Mid-North Community Committee. In the event one of these youngsters is committed to a correctional institution, members of the Committee continue to maintain contact with him or her while the youngster is in the institution. Periodic visits are made to institutions in order to give these young people the feeling that their neighbors are interested in their welfare. When the offender is ready to be released, the Mid-North Community Committee assists in formulating plans for parole. Efforts are made to assist the youngster in school adjustment or in securing employment. In addition, the Committee has provided similar services for adult offenders, some of whom attend regular meetings, and assume important responsibilities in helping the committee carry on its delinquency prevention program. Thus, these offenders have status in the conventional world by virtue of their acceptance by the members of the community and other local residents.

Many other types of activities are carried on by the Mid-North Community Committee to help make this a better community. Daily, local residents come to the Center for advice, information, and assistance in dealing with delinquency and related social problems.

An interesting illustration of how the Committee involves the participation of local residents in its community program is through social events and fundraising activities. For example, the Mid-North Community Committee has sponsored a 3-day Art and Fun Fair on Webster Avenue. Local men and women served pizza, sausage, and expresso coffee. Exhibited on the streets along the walls of buildings were paintings by artists from the neighborhood and adjoining areas. This was a new and unique event attended by over 5000 people who had an enjoyable time. Most important of all, the Committee raised approximately $1500 to help carry on its program.

The Committee's budget in 1977 was approximately $37,500. Of this amount $6500 was allocated by the Chicago Area Project.

Without question, the residents of this neighborhood believe that the Mid-North Community Committee is a constructive force in preventing delinquency and making the community a better place in which to live.

For example, the number of cases handled by the youth officers has been appreciably reduced to approximately 100 per year and the number of petitions on delinquency filed with the Juvenile Court have been reduced to approximately 10 to 15 each year. Of course, the Committee cannot fully solve many of the serious problems in the community, but it constantly seeks solutions cooperatively with the local schools, churches, industries, and institutions.

In recent years the work of this Committee has been greatly strengthened and enhanced with the active participation of many men from local business and industry. These individuals constitute the Committee's "Business Advisory Council." They raise funds, provide jobs, and support the program in many other ways.

In 1976, this Committee assumed responsibility for the operation of Camp Lange, a 26-acre site on a small lake near Michigan City, Indiana. Title to this property, purchased in the early 1940s by the Russell Square Community Committee, which has since gone out of existence, was given to the Chicago Area Project, the umbrella organization that encourages and supports community committees in Chicago.

Under the leadership of the MNCC, the camp program thus has continuity and serves children from many low-income areas of the city.

THE QUINCY STORY

About 5 years after the Chicago Area Project started, citizens in other parts of the state began to hear of Clifford Shaw's ideas and strategy for community development. Shaw often addressed groups all over the state on problems of delinquency, and his humane views and recommendations for dealing with the problems became widely known. When the superintendent for the Downstate Division for Delinquency Prevention resigned, Shaw was asked to become acting superintendent. He was reluctant to accept broader administrative responsibilities, but he finally yielded and accepted the challenge with the understanding that he would do so for about a year or until a successor could be employed. During this period he met with the downstate staff of delinquency prevention workers and spent most of his time speaking and training the workers. But some of the workers were skeptical of Shaw's self-help ideas. One such disbeliever was George Parsons, a worker in Herrin, Illinois in "Bloody Williamson County." "Your ideas won't work," Parsons told Shaw, "they are impractical and not feasible," he added. Shaw simply said, "George, all I ask is that you try the idea of enlisting people in Herrin and see what happens."

Always ready to accept a challenge, Parsons proceeded to talk to leaders in Herrin. One of them, Lan Haney, an attorney and later county judge, responded favorably and said that Shaw's ideas made sense. Encouraged by this attitude, Parsons soon found that people responded, most of all the offenders. Before long, a thriving organization of residents became a vital force in town and the incidence of delinquency was reduced. Parsons soon became a true believer and carried on his work with missionary zeal. His spirit was contagious and other downstate workers started to promote their work on the basis of Area Project principles—Porfi Picchi in Rockford, Jack Hunter in Rock Island—Moline, and George Withey in Springfield, among others. After a few years Withey was appointed downstate superintendent and Shaw continued as a consultant.

In 1951 Frank Baker, a downstate worker, met Mrs. Fabiola Moorman, head of the Moorman Manufacturing Company, a firm that produced livestock feed. Mrs. Moorman and her family foundation were interested in supporting programs in the fields of education, mental health, and community development. When she was introduced to Shaw and learned of his methods she asked for assistance in establishing a similar program in Quincy. Accordingly, the Moorman Foundation made a grant of $45,000 to the Chicago Area Project for the purpose of organizing the Quincy Area Project and to support similar ventures in Danville and some neighborhoods in Chicago.

Shaw chose Parsons as the community organizer for Quincy and in 1952 Parsons moved to this 130-year-old town along the Mississippi River across from Missouri. He found that Quincy, with a population of 60,000 had a high rate of commitments to the state training school. Since most of the delinquents came from four low-income neighborhoods he decided to select one of these four for the first venture. Simultaneously, he was contacting people in the underworld areas, red-light and vice districts, as well as the leaders representing the many diversified types of industries. As a newcomer he was at first suspected by the townspeople. The hoods thought he was an undercover agent, the police suspected he might be a dope peddler, agency people regarded him as a maverick, and the middle-class people weren't sure of his role. But word gets around quickly in a small town and people started to compare notes. Finally as Parsons' position was clarified, he was able to initiate action. From the leaders in industry he formed a board of directors to head the Quincy Area Project, which provided seed money to local residents to organize into neighborhood committees. Within a few years, four committees were organized in the disadvantaged areas and they continue to function actively to this day. In addition the committees have organized a federation that engages in social action to improve services or to deal with citywide issues affecting the residents in the low-income areas.

It was this Project that started a program in 1970 to intervene in the drug culture of Quincy. An organization, "Acid Rescue," has pioneered in the establishment of crisis centers, drop-in centers, residential centers, information centers, and street drug analysis. This program has substantially reduced commitments to correctional institutions and brought about constructive improvements in neighborhood life.

THE FEDERATION OF COMMUNITY COMMITTEES

In 1943 five community committees met to discuss common problems and agreed to join together to form the Chicago Federation of Community Committees. These committees were the Hegewisch Community Committee, the Near Northwest Community Committee, the South Side Community Committee, and the West Side Community Committee.

The purpose for establishing the Federation was to promote the common interest of its affiliates, to serve as a medium for exchange of knowledge about the task of dealing with delinquency on the neighborhood level, to establish a means by which committees could cooperate with one another in obtaining such public facilities and opportunities for the youth of each participating locality, and to eliminate some of the economic and social handicaps under which delinquency areas suffer.

As new committees were organized in later years by the Chicago Area Project, they became affiliated with the Federation. Today 16 such local organizations participate in this citywide endeavor. The Federation, under the leadership of Ray Raymond, one of our district supervisors, meets monthly, discusses problems and issues concerning delinquency prevention and rehabilitation as well as techniques for raising funds and recruiting volunteers. They exchange ideas on activities and programs for youth and community improvement and sponsor workshops and training seminars. At the Federation's Annual Dinner, which is attended by about 500 members and friends of the organization, awards are presented to outstanding volunteers and professional workers, including the Clifford R. Shaw Award, which is presented to a leader who has made a distinctive contribution to Area Project work.

Chapter 9

THE STORY OF AN INDIGENOUS LEADER

The story told in this chapter by a former "unofficial" delinquent is typical of the experiences of many boys in some of the low-income neighborhoods in Chicago who later became indigenous leaders in neighborhood organizations for the prevention of delinquency.

The following story (written about 10 years ago) describes first what it means to grow up in an ethnic community, the personal and family problems encountered in this situation, and second, it illustrates how this person's talents and leadership abilities were later utilized in a significant enterprise that the author has described in: *Organizing Against Crime: Redeveloping the Neighborhood* (Sorrentino, 1977).

This "community venture," as my author-friend has referred to it, has been a thrilling experience in my life. Viewed in contrast with the hard, rugged yet adventurous life of my childhood and youth, it is a sunrise emerging out of a dark cloud. But, before telling about this venture of ours and what it has meant to me and many others in my neighborhood, I think it is appropriate to give an account of my early life.

I was born within the shadow of Hull House, just east of Halsted Street on what is now known as Cabrini Street and across from where the Juvenile Detention Home was located.

My parents were Italian immigrants who came to this country while they were single. My mother's parents had passed away in Italy and her sister and brother-in-law sent for her to marry my father, then an eligible bachelor. My father had been in this country for some years, working as a transient railroad worker, traveling throughout the country. Today he is a janitor. My father is a very simple man and a very illiterate person; he was born in the hills of Calabria, where in his youth he was a shepherd. Even now without much prompting we can get him to sing his mountaineer songs of old sunny Italy and play the accordion as well. Sung in Calabrian dialect with a distinct nasal intonation, the tempo of his chants sound like a cross between the Greek songs and Irish jigs.

The simple folk pattern of the mountain peasants of Calabria are forever ingrained on his personality, as evidenced by the fact that although he has lived in a big city like Chicago for over forty years, his mode of life has changed little. Even with the most recent urban wonder—television—(to which he has a magical attraction and sits by the hour watching most avidly "Gorgeous George" and his other wrestling idols), he is still a good simple-hearted peasant. After a hard day's work his only pleasure and care is to come home, preferring spaghetti and wine to other dishes, and depending on a Parodi cigar or his corncob pipe for the after-dinner relaxations.

My mother and father were married in 1912 and I was born exactly one year later. My two sisters were born a few years later and after an interval of 17½ years my brother was born.

My father has an odd and peculiar way of remembering my birthday and continued existence. When I was born he worked in a factory where a heavy iron object fell on his toe.

Ignoring the doctors he treated himself and, as a result, a peculiar growth developed. Since, over the years, he has attended to this growth himself by cutting it down with a saw, he can always remember that the accident occurred on the day of my birth. Suggesting a doctor of course is sheer heresy, for his sense of self-sufficiency would be slighted.

My mother had a more urban background, coming from Catanzaro, a city in Calabria. She was more alert to the ways of the city, did the planning and thinking in our house and managed with firmness all the affairs of our household. She also worked in tailor shops as an armhole baster, but even so our income was small. In addition we had two boarders in those early days, men who were recent newcomers from the old country and who sought lodgings with their "paesani." My grandfather lived with us during this time until he died several years later. My mother died recently.

My recollections of those early days are one of constant moving about, seldom staying in one dwelling for more than a year or two, but always remaining in the heart of the Italian colony. All of these three-flat or tenement buildings we lived in were about the same, so that our moving about changed our scenery very little. It was the same colorless pattern.

In another building we lived in, a moonshine still was in operation in the basement and the second floor was used for storage and living quarters. We lived on the third floor. The police raided the second floor one day and we had to help the family that was raided dispose of the alcohol by pouring it down our kitchen sink and toilet bowl. I was glad to help too because my playmate, a cross-eyed kid we nicknamed "78 Eyes" was the landlord's son.

Since my parents were not always regularly employed, we at times had to rely upon charity dispensed by some Catholic agency. It was during this time that I learned to eat raw oatmeal —and like it.

A seriously religious woman, my mother registered me in a parochial school, where I became an altar boy. But first I want to tell of my nursery school experience. Since my parents went to work early, leaving the house at 7 A.M., we children were taken to a nearby charitable Catholic nursery where we remained until school opened and returned after school until our parents came to call for us.

The nursery was a pleasant place and we were treated kindly by the Irish women who operated it. I remember in particular a big fat woman, the superintendent, who was tender-hearted and who seemed to understand me well, although others felt she was hard and cruel. While at the nursery one day, Ben and I did a little exploring around the place when the matronly eyes of the teachers were not fixed on us. This was when we were about eleven years old. We knew the nursery had a veritable mine of donated objects and playthings stored in the barn, so we went out on little adventures to satisfy our childish curiosity.

I have since forgotten many of the things we marvelled at, but there were two huge books which made a lasting impression. One, *The Life of William McKinley,* was the book I robbed. Ben grabbed a huge volume entitled *Modern Library Book.* In thumbing through the pages of my book, which among other things gave a vivid account of the assassination of President McKinley, Ben suggested that we trade books because that account had a greater fascination for him. It was indeed a happy exchange for this *Modern Library Book* whetted my appetite for learning, and greatly stirred my curiosity and imagination. Here were pictures of butterflies and birds, discussions of such subjects as biology, geography, history, and mathematics, and condensations of great novels. It can well be said that this marked the real beginning of my intellectual development.

It seemed that my adjustment in "sister school," as we called it, did not proceed according to an orderly pattern. I was frequently punished there for misbehavior and after several years I had to be transferred to a public school. All in all, though, I liked school and got along well in my studies. I played hooky a few times, but this was merely to attend a few choice movies.

Much of our time as children was spent on the street more than any other place. Along with the kids in my gang I was involved in a lot of activities which no doubt were delinquent. We had completely free rein over our activities and we would wander around in and out of our immediate community to go junking or shining shoes or selling newspapers. Of these activities I engaged in junking more persistently. We would tear lead pipes, wiring, and other metals out of abandoned buildings and sell them to the junk man. Quite frequently we would steal car parts and sell them to older fellows in the neighborhood—many of whom became members of our famous "42 Gang." We specialized in stealing "motor meters" as they were then called—elegant contraptions used on cars in those days as a sort of radiator cap.

Taking things seemed to be second nature. Practically every kid I knew engaged in stealing with regularity. We directed our attention to one candy store in particular. We knew the proprietor's habits and when he leaned under his counter, we could easily snatch the five-cent size cookie boxes, stuff them into our pockets and then march over to church to serve mass.

During this time—I was about twelve years old—there were two gangs on our street—the "good" gang and the "bad" gang. Actually there was little difference, if any, between the two groups. One day as we were walking through an alley and spotted a car that had already been stripped by the older fellows, we proceeded to take the smaller parts which had not been looted. Looking in the glove compartment, one of my playmates spotted a wedding picture which he wanted to take. I insisted that it be left behind. I guess by this time I was getting a little soft.

As we got older and outgrew the nursery school, we would be left on our own after school hours. As the oldest child, I was responsible for the other children and was given possession of our house key. Certain playmates would come to our house to play. One day one of these boys stole my father's gold watch and when my parents discovered the theft I was blamed and roundly punished. I explained that I suspected a certain boy and after questioning him sternly, the boy confessed. He had hidden the watch by dangling it on a string under the coal chute lid near the sidewalk of his home. Another time a playmate stole my parents total savings—$95—an incident which was a really heartbreaking scene. After much wailing and tearing of hair, my mother calmed down and we proceeded on a systematic search of those playmates who had recently been in our home. Luckily for me, we finally found the culprit and the money was restored.

As we kids got older I guess we became more bold and daring for we seldom passed up an opportunity to steal something. I remember vividly a fire which destroyed a doughnut factory near our home. After the firemen left we proceeded to raid this factory, coming out loaded with great quantities of cocoa and sugar which we disposed of by selling to local grocers. On occasion we would make the rounds of barns where local peddlers stored their horses and wagons. We would break in and feast upon bananas and other fruit and carry away whatever else we could.

Horses remind me of numerous nauseating scenes of my childhood. Whenever a horse died it was left in the alley for an unreasonably long time. You would expect that either a private scavenger or the city authorities would be interested in removing the rotting carcass immediately—but no, it was left around for days. What a putrid mess those horses looked, especially on summer days with millions of flies swarming around the carcass! The news spread far and near and whoever discovered the still and ugly beast would be sure to invite the other kids to marvel at it.

Our play was not entirely of this sort, however. We engaged in a wide variety of street games, including softball and handball. We would also attend the local community centers on occasion, but not regularly. Of the local ꜰgencies the one that exerted a lasting influence in my life was the nursery school. It offered contact with people outside my neighborhood and it instilled habits and ideas which had a beneficial effect on my personality.

My parents, of course, were unaware of the things we did in the streets. My mother, who was very strict, would often warn me not to go with "bad company." I knew better than to ever take stolen articles home unless I could give a legitimate accounting.

Reflecting now on all the stealing I did as a boy, I can appreciate the fact that I was never caught. Had I been apprehended and hauled into Court, these activities would have likely been diagnosed as "criminal tendencies" and the acts of a maladjusted or psychopathic individual. I am indeed lucky that I was never caught, as were others, who upon completion of their "training" in the State School and reformatory merely seemed to come out better prepared for a further life of crime.

At the age of fourteen I entered high school. After school I had a newspaper route and for awhile I worked in a drugstore, thinking for a time that I might become a pharmacist. Since I could not sleep much at night, I became a omnivorous reader, overly preoccupied I'm afraid, with pulp magazines until I developed a taste for better literature as my work progressed in high school.

I think I was a good student. I applied myself conscientiously to my studies and finished high school in three years, making the honor roll. Here one of the rich and constructive experiences of my life started when I became closely associated with Seymour Nash, a Jewish lad. He was intellectually inclined, read a lot and appreciated the arts and finer things of life. He influenced me a great deal along intellectual lines. I mixed well with other persons and groups, however, and spent the usual time in high school sports and extracurricular activities. I was especially active on the school paper and seemed to be interested in journalism to such an extent that the class historian predicted (wrongly) that I was to become a sportswriter.

There was one sour note, however, during the last year of high school which continued over to my junior college days and after. During this time a "notorious gangster" (the newspaper called him), John (no relation), was prominent in the newspapers. He was alleged to have killed federal police, operated vice rackets and other notorious activities. Jokingly, the people would ask me in and out of school, "Say, are you related to John"? There was jest to this query, but nevertheless I became rather self-conscious about the fact that in the minds of non-Italians we Italians were regarded more or less as gangsters, murderers, and lawless creatures. This was the beginning of my feelings of inferiority. They became more pronounced as I entered the city junior college where Italians were a minority. As a result, the few Italian students would tend to form a clique. By being together we felt more at home.

Then I entered a period of lofty idealism. I felt that I could prepare myself for a significant place in the scheme of things in our great city by studying law. In the interim I fell in love with a girl of Scandinavian background, but my association with her merely developed further my feelings of inferiority. I became more conscious of my Italian background and the tie was severed for this and other reasons. I became convinced that being Italian you start out life by having two strikes against you.

I had to struggle through school. Frequently I was unable to purchase the required school materials. I was poorly dressed and never had sufficient money for those things that young people require as they go through this stage. Although I had a sense of adequacy and self-confidence as a student because I could do satisfactory work, I was becoming increasingly aware of my poor background, and feelings of insecurity were starting to crop up.

Mingling with hundreds of students from other parts of the city and exposed more and more to life outside my community,

I began to wonder about my future. While I was sure I wanted to be a lawyer, I had all kinds of anxieties and wondered how I was going to make the grade. These were not imagined thoughts, for in reality it was a long and difficult climb before I could call myself a successful and established lawyer. As a member of a minority group and a resident of a slum area, I began to realize that success could not be achieved in the idealistic manner portrayed in the books.

While taking a course in sociology we were required to work on a practical project. I was assigned to do volunteer work at Hull House where I passed out soap and towels at the shower room and supervised activities in the gameroom. It was here that I met Mark Alderman, an associate of Clifford R. Shaw, who had come into our community to preach a new gospel in social welfare. He asked me questions about our community, its background and the problems of our people. He talked to others and soon after we got together in a group. We were all of the same opinion with regard to the basic problems of our community. We sensed deeply that our area had a bad reputation and that being Italian was a handicap in trying to get up in the world. Inspired by the informal talks, we decided to form a permanent group, calling ourselves the "I Fratelli Guidanti"— The Guiding Brothers—a nucleus that was to blaze the trail for an eventual civic and community improvement program.

Mr. Alderman told us about the Chicago Area Project, a program proposed by Mr. Shaw which grew out of his studies and research regarding the problem of delinquency. Mr. Shaw spoke to our group and told us of this history of delinquency in our community. As he rolled out a map of Chicago he pointed out that our area—the area surrounding the Loop— also had a high rate of delinquency when other immigrant groups resided there; assuring us that there was no foundation whatsoever that the Italians were criminally inclined, as the newspaper and movies would have us believe. He talked about the importance of self-help, expressing great faith in the ability of our people to solve their problems if they would band together and work cooperatively with their local leaders and institutions.

We were thrilled and deeply moved by these ideas and impressed with the genuine and sincere spirit in which they were presented. This was the first time that anyone had come into our midst with such a positive and hopeful approach; one that provided a significant place for us. Here was a simple yet very appealing proposal. This was something we could help create and build and feel that we belonged to. It is true that we had notions about civic work and community welfare long before we had heard about the Chicago Area Project, but we did not have the method or outside help needed to start us on our way. The Area Project was thus the real answer to our earlier hopes and desires.

A community council composed of the older men of our neighborhood was organized, while we younger men were banded together as the Guiding Brothers. We joined forces with the Council, however, and became an integral part of this venture. A few of our younger men served on the Council's Board of Directors; others were employed on the project, while still others helped by volunteering on the community newspaper which the Council started.

When the reorganization took place and we younger men organized the West Side Community Committee, a number of the Guiding Brothers were very active in its direction and development, but always remaining in the background in formal leadership roles. We had a sort of unofficial pact among us that we would not hold major offices in the group. We felt that since those of us who had sparked this movement were thoroughly committed to its principles, we would be conferring some recognition and honor on the newcomers. As an illustration: one day a young man, a truck driver who had heard about our work from a friend, dropped in to look us over. Apparently he became interested, for shortly after he started to come around, frequently stopping to chat about our developing program and volunteering to wash the windows or perform odd jobs. This chap had been in our midst a short time when it was tacitly agreed by the older members that he should be our next president.

This procedure was effective for many reasons. First it gave these fellows recognition and a feeling of belonging. Secondly, these fellows recruited other persons whom they knew. Finally, it gave them an excellent opportunity to learn how to conduct meetings, express themselves, and learn more intimately about our problems.

For me, participation in our community committee opened new vistas. It made me feel proud to know that our Italian people could work together for such noble objectives. As we started to accomplish things and see what we could do as a united group, I began to lose that feeling of inferiority. I could begin to joke about my name now because for every "notorious ganster" we could show a hundred young men engaged in civic work—something that we couldn't do before.

Before long we realized that what we were doing in our own neighborhood had far-reaching ramifications. Our work put us in touch with the larger community and we started to meet a lot of persons and groups in the city. We had dealings with foundations, associations of commerce, councils of social agencies, the Community Fund, and a large number of public and private agencies. Occasionally we were asked to speak to women's clubs, civic associations, and colleges.

We thus got a lot of good experience in the process of meeting and talking with others in the city. Probably more important, we started to see ourselves in a different light. We began to develop a greater spirit of self-confidence because we soon realized we could make a positive contribution to our community and city.

After a few years we also realized that our neighborhood was related to other neighborhoods and other human beings regardless of race, color, or creed. In the course of our work we met Mexicans, Negroes, Greeks, Jews, and other ethnic groups and joined with them in various civic affairs. We learned that we had common problems, many of them transcending our own immediate neighborhood, and that we all ought to work together to try to solve our problems.

Encouraged and helped by the Chicago Area Project, we thus took the initiative in 1945, to organize the Chicago Federation of Community Committees, which for years was chaired by N. E. Nelson, a Swede, and a member of the West Side Community Committee. Later I became president of this Federation which is composed of delegates of sixteen neighborhood organizations, all of them fostered and aided by the Chicago Area Project. The Federation is thus the collective instrument of self-help of the citizens' organizations in Chicago. All of us —Italians, Negroes, Mexicans, Poles, Jews, Irish—yet really all Americans—come together frequently to exchange ideas and experiences regarding our community problems, aid one another in this mutual task and work cooperatively in dealing with public officials and other agencies on matters related to our problems and objectives.

Because of my experience in these enterprises I am called upon to talk on the problem of delinquency, to represent our Committee and Federation in public hearings. I also have been a member of the Delinquency Prevention Committee of the Chicago Bar Association.

I can honestly say that these experiences were responsible for charting my future in entirely new directions. Without these constructive influences I'm afraid I might have weakened under the beckoning gestures and direct invitations of the non-conventional world, which are mighty enticing for the young lawyer. When opportunities in the larger society are inaccessible to him, he may have no other recourse but to accept them and adapt himself to the way of that world.

As a participant in this human drama it has been possible for me to drive away those earlier feelings of inferiority and insecurity. It has been a valuable training school for me because it gave me a chance to express myself, to learn to think and work with others, to become more thoroughly imbued with the democratic way of life; to work with youngsters and adults who have been in trouble and in various ways to help them; to organize groups and plan and promote all kinds of programs and activities; to work shoulder to shoulder with other minority groups in the city.

I believe that as a result I am today better prepared as an individual to solve my personal and family problems. I am a better Catholic too, because I have seen the teachings of Christ translated into action. I am better trained and equipped to pursue my profession. I am better prepared to participate as a citizen in the affairs of my city, state and nation. And I believe I am imbued too with those views and attitudes which would seem to be necessary in the establishment of a world society, based upon those principles of humanity which are enunciated in all the great religions of the world.

Chapter 10

MUNICIPAL AND TOWNSHIP
YOUTH ORGANIZATIONS

LEGISLATIVE AUTHORITY

The trend toward higher rates of juvenile delinquency and crime has now attained serious proportions and demands sustained community attention, not only from private citizens but also governmental agencies as well. In recent years local governments have also begun to establish youth and community programs or ordinances, especially in suburban areas. Financed with public funds, representing public commitment to provide leadership and resources in behalf of youth, such programs, however, should not substitute for but complement any voluntary or public planning agencies and other groups concerned with youth problems, needs, and opportunities.

The structure of the governmental agency may be a municipal commission, or a township commission. In addition, many states have state commissions or youth boards performing delinquency prevention functions. In this chapter, however, we deal only with the former. Whatever its structure may be as determined by local authorities through official legal action, it is desirable that it should have its own identity and should be lodged at the highest possible level in government. The agency should be bipartisan, having the broadest possible representation and have policymaking functions. (In the appendix are reproduced three sample copies of Youth Commission Ordinances. Evanston and Moline are examples of municipal youth commissions; and Lyons Township is an example of a township committee.)

Of course, the establishment of a local youth commission, or a township commission, has to be supported by the local responsible authorities such as the mayor or president and the majority of the council members, supervisors, or commissioners of the particular municipality or township. The endorsement of the chief of police, judicial body, and other local officials is also desired for a cooperative effort.

The broad purposes of a youth commission assigned the task of delinquency prevention might well include the following:

1. Define and document youth problems in order to establish a factual base for the development of programs.
2. Recommend and put into effect those measures most suitable to supplement and aid in coordinating the work of existing institutions or agencies for the prevention of individual and social deprivation.
3. Stimulate and encourage effective use of existing institutions or agencies and the development of new or additional programs to meet the needs of children and youth and their families.
4. Promote opportunities for advancement of the moral, physical, mental, and social well-being of youth.

To achieve these objectives, the youth commission should actively seek out and recommend measures in attempting to deal with youth problems, utilizing all possible public and private resources. In general, the responsibility to provide continuing direct services to the individual and family should be with private agencies. However, in some communities where resources are inadequate, a local commission might provide direct services of its own.

Possible Functions

Ideally municipal or township commissions should not assume permanent responsibility for direct service programs. They may, however, elect to demonstrate projects that have clear terminal dates and provisions for being taken up by other agencies, or interim services where there is no other agency available to meet a present need. Direct services should be limited and, when appropriate, efforts should be made to secure an existing agency to undertake the task or suggest the creation of a new agency not under the auspices of the youth commission. However, in practice this does not always work out and the commission may decide to serve as an operating agency.

Examples of functions that may be carried out by youth commissions include the following:

1. Provide planning leadership that engages other public and private agencies and local communities.
2. Gather, organize, analyze, and share information about conditions affecting youth and families.
3. Carry on public education and information projects on delinquency.
4. Encourage existing agencies to innovate and revitalize their programs in relation to needs.
5. Facilitate communication and contacts between local communities and outside resources, that is, funding research, and the like.
6. Develop and improve communications and relationships between local people, institutions, and organizations.

7. Promote coordination and cooperation among community resources.
8. Advise government officials, other agencies, and the general public of needed action.
9. Organize and implement training programs for personnel in the field of youth work in cooperation with other agencies.
10. Obtain and disseminate information regarding enforcement of local and state laws insofar as they concern the protection and welfare of youth.
11. Encourage closer cooperation between employers, labor, schools, churches, recreation commissions, state and local employment bureaus, service clubs, and other public and private agencies to stimulate employment for youth at fair wages and encourage sound youth programs.

Although *action* should be the goal of a youth commission, an important tool might well be research and careful planning. Essential in this connection is to conduct surveys and studies of the community and of specific problems; assist in the development and establishment of uniform statistics and procedures for youth crime, delinquency, and neglect; and gather and disseminate other relevant information that may reflect trends pertinent to youth welfare.

ORGANIZATIONAL STRUCTURE

The structure of a governmental agency such as a municipal or township youth commission will depend, for the most part, on basic authority, the level of government at which the administrative structure is located, and the purpose for which the agency is established. Members of these youth agencies may be appointed by the local chief executive. Such membership should be broadly representative of the community and designed to foster maximum and effective participation. It should not be so large as to be unwieldy.

The size of the membership in youth commissions tends to vary accordingly with the community and seriousness of the problems facing the agency. Practice indicates that youth agencies vary in membership from 5 to 33. When the average membership is around 15, it should include the mayor or president, a juvenile officer or other members of the police department, and a member of the council. In addition to the appointed members, the youth board should have authority to use the services of such citizens that may be needed from time to time to assist subcommittees to carry out their assignments.

The term of office may be on a rotating basis to provide continuity of membership. The usual term of office may be about 3 years which would give a carryover membership of two-thirds.

The officers of the local youth agency may include the following:

1. President.
2. Vice-president.
3. Secretary–treasurer.
4. Any other officer that may be necessary.

A small number of officers is highly recommended to avoid overlapping of duties. All officers and the subcommittee chairperson should compose the executive committee. The initial chairperson of the youth board or commission should be appointed by the chief executive. Thereafter he or she may be appointed or be elected by the commission.

When a youth commission is legally authorized by local government, usually some funds are provided for its operation. The amount may vary from several hundred dollars at its inception to substantial sums as the program is developed and its value proven. The latter is especially necessary if an executive director is to be employed. Larger communities have found it necessary to employ an executive director to administer the programs and policies set by the commission. Staff employed by the youth commission should have the experience and educational background related to its function.

To utilize the talents of the members making up the youth commission effectively, each member might be assigned as chairperson of a subcommittee. He or she should be encouraged to expand the committee by canvassing the community and seeking the assistance of volunteers who would assist in carrying out the functions of the particular committee. In so doing, the general membership will increase many times over, thereby spreading the philosophy, need, and efforts of the youth commission. The chairperson of each subcommittee should report periodically to the chairperson of the organization to discuss the progress of the committee.

One area that is often overlooked in the formation of youth commissions and subcommittees is the involvement of youth. It seems that there is a reluctance to appoint teenagers to top-level youth agencies where the membership is large. There is a feeling that youth could not make a contribution although their involvement could provide insight to youth and community. It could prove beneficial to include on the youth agency as an ex-officio member the president of the senior class in the local community high school, for example. Youth resent being dictated to. They want opportunities to voice their opinions. All citizens' groups should provide adequate channels of communication with the youth of the community.

SUBCOMMITTEES

The number of subcommittees that may be created will depend on the size of the organization, the number of volunteers, and its needs. Following is a list of subcommittees that should be considered although they by no means represent the total that may be created to meet a need.

1. *Survey:* The function of this subcommittee should be to obtain data that would assist the local authorities and other subcommittees. This information may be obtained through a door-to-door survey utilizing the assistance of various service organizations such as the Lions, P.T.A., Kiwanis, and other school and church programs. A questionnaire may be distributed. In areas where telephone, electric, gas, and water bills are mailed periodically, arrangements may be made to include the questionnaires with the bill.

2. *Recreation:* Its function should be to determine what recreational facilities are being used or made available in a particular community and to determine to what extent the recreational agencies need assistance in conducting the program that they are offering to the youngsters.

3. *Publicity:* It should keep the public informed of the agency's activities and disseminate information related to youth.

4. *Finance:* The youth commission treasurer should be chairperson of this committee. This committee should prepare the annual budget and submit it to local authorities for approval. The committee should also take aggressive steps to augment funds provided by the local authorities with contributions from interested citizens if so authorized by local legislative action.

5. *Program:* Its function should be to provide diversity in the schedule of meetings and programs, particularly where volunteers are involved. Its scope should cover enlightenment, fundraising if indicated, and some entertainment.

6. *Cases:* It should accept and screen referred cases from the court, police, and schools; secure sponsors to work with accepted cases; and refer cases for counseling.

7. *Employment:* It should study employment needs of youth and job opportunities in the community.

8. *Adult Education:* Its purpose should be to sponsor programs at which qualified speakers would discuss problems of youth misbehavior and subjects of a more positive nature.

The above committees are merely suggestions. Many others may be appointed by the chairperson depending on the nature of local needs and problems.

It is imperative that youth commissions continuously work in close cooperation with all other public and private agencies and organizations working on behalf of the youth. Of special importance is a close working relationship with all existing physical social planning groups. Experience has demonstrated that interdisciplinary collaboration is essential to success and that no one professional group in and of itself has all the answers to the complex problems affecting children and young people of today.

YOUTH COMMISSIONS IN ILLINOIS

Since 1950, there has been a great proliferation of municipal youth commissions and township committees on youth in localities throughout Illinois, especially in the more populous, urban communities of northern Illinois. These organizations were created in response to a new situation: as population increased and other social changes took place in many suburban communities, the volume of delinquency greatly increased. As more and more youngsters were coming to the attention of the police, it was clear that many of the suburbs had meager, if not nonexistent, resources to provide for the needs of the increasing adolescent population. Juvenile police officers often had no services or programs to refer children in need of counseling or guidance. In the absence of community-based services, they often had no alternative but to refer delinquents to the Juvenile Court, and hence a number of such offenders ended up in the state's correctional institutions. Gradually many middle-class communities then became interested in diverting children away from the juvenile justice system.

When the Illinois Youth Commission, the state agency having responsibility for juvenile corrections as well as prevention of delinquency, was established in 1953, one of the purposes was to assist local communities in organizing programs for youth welfare and delinquency control. At that time this agency had over 100 community workers who met with and advised local officials and residents in different localities. The institutional forms that were created to deal with youth problems were either community committees or youth councils and later municipal youth commissions and township committees on youth. In 1963, Representative Donald Moore introduced legislation (H.B. 1180 and amended in 1971 as H.B. 739) in the General Assembly, giving legal sanction to the Board of Town Auditors to establish and authorize tax funds for youth work. Originally designed for communities with over a million population, the legislation as later amended, sanctioned and authorized all townships in Illinois to establish committees on youth if they chose to do so.

As a result of this legislation and the state's encouragement, approximately 50 such committees are operating in Illinois spending close to $3 million in tax funds for youth work for delinquency prevention.

Today staff members from the Illinois Commission on Delinquency Prevention serve as consultants and resource persons to municipal commissions and township committees on youth. Eugene Wroblewski was instrumental recently in organizing the Association of Township Commissions.

Chapter 11

EVALUATION OF NEIGHBORHOOD ORGANIZATIONS

PROBLEMS AND GUIDELINES

The effectiveness of any delinquency prevention program should, of course, be appraised—both on a long- and short-term basis. However, there are many problems in evaluting such programs. Even relatively reliable data are difficult to secure and it is virtually impossible to ascertain the relationship between trends and specific programs. Conscientious attempts to secure reliable data with reference to Area Project programs has not furnished results that will stand up under rigorous scientific scrutiny.

In several communities where a program has been in operation for a number of years, there has been a downward trend in the volume of delinquency. The difficulty is in interpreting what this trend means because the data fluctuate widely in small areas and because even if it can be established that a decrease has taken place, it may have been due to other influences in the community or in changes in administrative procedure.

Notwithstanding these difficulties, Helen Witmer, in a study for the U.S. Children's Bureau (Witmer & Tufts, 1954), made perhaps the most balanced evaluation of neighborhood committees:

1. Residents in low-income areas can and have organized themselves into effective working units for promoting and conducting welfare programs.
2. These community organizations have been stable and enduring. They raise funds, administer them well, and adapt the programs to local needs.
3. Local talent, otherwise untapped, has been discovered and utilized. Local leadership has been mobilized in the interest of children's welfare.

There are still ways, however, of appraising the value of local neighborhood programs.

When the people of a neighborhood band together and work collectively in a community welfare program, new and basic resources are brought to bear on the problem. As residents work on behalf of their children and community, new and positive attitudes are formed as a result of this concern and action. This means, therefore, that the child is living in a new situation and responding to new constructive social influences. It seems reasonable to assume that these influences and the improvements in general living conditions, which the residents are able to effect, operate both for the prevention of delinquency and the treatment of delinquents (Sorrentino, 1959).

Such constructive programs as these are not substitutes for a more objective evaluation. It should be stressed that methods employed not only by neighborhood committees but in all welfare programs should be reexamined and critically evaluated from time to time. Without continuous experimentation and testing, new methods of treatment and prevention are not likely to be developed.

Another practical way to evaluate the neighborhood organization is to annually review and assess the program in accordance with its stated goals and objectives.

It might also be necessary to evaluate the organization and its program in the event of drastic changes in leadership, organizational structure, or crisis in the community.

Since such evaluations are desirable and indeed necessary, it should be understood, therefore, that each community organization have its purpose clearly stated in writing (constitution and bylaws) that forms the basis of its specific program objectives. Such documents are necessary in order to review and evaluate the program periodically.

In such an evaluation the person making the analysis should consider the adequacy of the organization's administrative staff, policies and program, buildings and equipment, community relationships, and, above all, records. Further details of these broad guidelines are described in the statement on Standards for Neighborhood Committees discussed later in this chapter.

In addition to these guidelines, there are key questions that should be focused on.

1. Is the organization composed primarily of local residents who are representatives of the neighborhood?
2. To what extent is the organization operating on the basis of its objectives and goals?
3. What concrete evidence is there that progress is being made in achieving its goals relative to membership, program, fundraising, and the like?
4. Does the organization have a significant number of volunteers assuming responsibility for various aspects of the program?
5. Does the organization actually engage in working with predelinquents and delinquents and what success or failure is it encountering? What are target groups and how are they identified? What programs and services are provided as delinquency prevention measures?

6. Does the organization operate on the basis of the principles of democracy and sound human relations?
7. Does the organization give accountability of its work, program, and funds raised to the members and to the public?

These and other specific questions can be used as a starting point in evaluating the work of a community organization.

The following pages list those items relating to organizations, programs, and services that can be used as guidelines for securing some of the data that may be helpful in evaluating neighborhood committees.

In Appendix 1 is a sample copy of suggested bylaws for a neighborhood or community committee, followed by a sample of the oath of office administered when officers are installed.

STANDARDS FOR NEIGHBORHOOD COMMITTEES

I. *Objectives and Functions*
Each neighborhood committee should have its purpose clearly stated in writing (constitution and/or bylaws) that forms the basis of its specific program objectives. The purpose and objectives should be reviewed periodically for critical analysis and evaluation of the program.

Each neighborhood committee is to be engaged in nonpolitical, nonracial, and nonsectarian neighborhood welfare work with special reference to the treatment of delinquents and the prevention of delinquency and is expected to:
A. Work with juvenile and other offenders as individuals or as members of groups or gangs, attempt to redirect their activities into constructive channels, and aid them in their efforts to achieve a satisfactory place in the conventional life of the community.
B. Promote social action programs involving large seg-

ments of the total population to combat conditions known to contribute to delinquency.

C. Develop and promote programs among the residents to strengthen community life and improve neighborhood conditions.

D. Aid and assist individuals and families in their efforts to deal with personal problems.

II. *Administration*

The neighborhood committee should have the kind of administration that will assure its successful operation and management in fulfilling its objectives and goals.

A. *Membership and Board of Directors.* Each committee should have a membership available to all the residents of the community which, at its annual meeting, will elect a Board of Directors. This Board should meet no less than eight times a year and should be selected on the basis of its interest and ability to assist in meeting the welfare problems of the community. There should be a policy expressed by the membership as to the length of term of Board membership. The members of the Board should be primarily residents who live in the area in which the committee operates.

B. *The membership of a neighborhood committee* is expected to participate in the program planning and execution, as well as in the formulation of policy.

C. *Officers.* The officers should be elected annually by the Board of Directors.

D. *Personnel Committee and Policies.* Among the standing committees of the Board of Directors, there shall be a Personnel Committee, the members of which shall formulate and recommend personnel policies to the Board. It is desirable that this committee represent the staff as well as the Board of Directors.

E. Each committee should be accountable for a public statement of income and expenditure. It should elect or appoint a treasurer whose reports should be audited annually. Solicitation programs for financial support should be planned carefully in accordance with currently accepted accounting practices and should include the necessary check to assure that all contributions are used in accordance with the desires of the contributors.

III. *Staff*

The committee through its officers or Board of Directors should employ or appoint staff members, if needed, and set forth their duties and responsibilities.

A. *Professional*

1. *Committee Executive.* Each neighborhood committee should have an executive with broad knowledge of community welfare service and with administrative skills and experience in community organization.

2. *Other Staff.* Other staff employed by the neighborhood committee should have a combination of training and experience so that they will have (a) knowledge of the social problems of the community, (b) ability to work with and maintain successful relationships with residents and co-workers, and (c) ability to work with and gain the confidence of delinquents and their groups. Each community committee that operates out of a facility should provide the necessary clerical and janitorial service.

3. *Specialists.* Specialists should meet the professional requirements of their respective fields.

B. *Volunteers—Part-time employees—Students*

1. Provision should be made for in-service training for volunteers and part-time instructors, group leaders, activity leaders, and counselors.

IV. *Committee Policies and Program*
   A. The program activities should be so planned, supervised, and executed to lead to the achievement of the specific objectives of the committee. The ratio of staff in the activities of the committee should be such as to assure the development of program in accordance with the purposes of the organization and to provide proper safeguards for the health, safety, and welfare of the participants.
   B. Through the widest possible participation of parents and other local residents, the neighborhood committee should seek to take action against those conditions in the neighborhood that directly contribute to delinquency or in other ways interfere with the normal development of children.
   C. The committee in developing programs for the treatment of delinquents and for the prevention of delinquency should utilize and involve as many of the residents as possible both in the formulation and in the execution of such programs. Special programs should be devised for groups of delinquents at the neighborhood level. Special adult education programs should provide the residents of the neighborhood with a better understanding of the problems of children and young people. Through joint action on the part of the residents, every effort should be made to improve the recreational, educational, and other community services to children and, in a like manner, foster the general physical and social improvement of the community.
   D. Each committee should have written intake policies and procedures setting forth clearly its method of accepting clientele.
   E. Each committee should have established and publicized geographic areas of operation.

V. *Building and Equipment*
  A. All buildings and equipment must conform to state
     and local building regulations and the requirements of
     state and local departments of health and fire preven-
     tion.
  B. The physical plant should be as well adapted to the
     program of the committee as possible. Budget provi-
     sions should be made to assure adequate upkeep of
     equipment and facilities in order to assure an attrac-
     tive and suitable atmosphere.
  C. Budget provision should be made to afford adequate
     insurance on buildings and equipment.

VI. *Community Relationships*
   It is recognized that the local community, either in the
   geographical or psychological sense, is vitally affected by
   citywide, national, and even world forces. Community relationships, therefore, must account for these wider influences on life.
  A. Neighborhood committees should represent a true
     cross section of the population to assure that the
     members of the committee will have a broad knowl-
     edge of the resources and problems of the area.
  B. The committees should work constructively and co-
     operatively with the other agencies and institutions of
     the community, utilizing all of the forces and facilities
     available in efforts to improve the services available to
     the residents. Each community committee should be-
     long and become active with its neighborhood or
     community planning council.
  C. Every committee should have a definite goal of utiliz-
     ing indigenous leadership in the neighborhood and of
     developing new leadership.
  D. The committee's function should be defined in terms
     of the community's need and its resources.
  E. The policy of each committee should include services
     to all the residents regardless of race, creed, color,

political affiliation, or nationality. It is understood, however, that committees organized to serve a specific group may give primary consideration to that group. (It is recognized that this is a means toward total integration in the community.)

VII. *Records*

A. The collection of records, statistical and narrative, to be of value to the neighborhood committee should be analyzed periodically as a basis for an evaluation in the planning of the program. Periodic analyses should be made of statistical or factual information relevant to the programs of the committee—that is, community socioeconomic facts, data on specific problems, and the like.

B. Interviews and narrative records should be kept as a means of recording steps in helping the people the committee serves. No committee should be placed or place itself in the position of violating the confidence of these people and such records should be kept confidential.

C. Statistical records of the committee should include:

   1. Indentifying data for each member or registrant, including such items as names, address, sex, and age.

   2. Group attendance records for each group with definite enrollment indicating participation in these groups.

   3. Monthly records of group activities, classified by type of groups, should be kept.

D. Neighborhood committees should keep brief, narrative records for all individual delinquents and groups, and should experiment with fuller narrative records for a limited number of individuals and groups.

Appendix 1*

BYLAWS FOR A NEIGHBORHOOD COMMITTEE

Article I: Name

The [*name of the corporation*] is a nonprofit organization located in the [*designate general area*].

Article II: Objectives

1. To enlist the talents and efforts of local residents and other civic-minded citizens of good moral character for the purpose of fostering and supporting programs for the prevention and treatment of juvenile delinquency and for the improvement of health, housing, and educational conditions, in order to make

*The following appendices present only suggestions concerning formalities, including legislation that might be used as a model outside Illinois. But "localism" would imply that these forms would be altered to fit unique circumstances in each case.

the community a better place in which to live, work, and pursue constructive business, commercial, and industrial enterprises.

2. To cultivate a social relationship, encourage closer personal acquaintance, and develop a friendly spirit of cooperation in the community.

3. To aid and assist in the general furtherance of community welfare as expressed in programs for the improvement of health, housing, juvenile corrections, adult education, and public information through the instrumentality and leadership of representative neighborhood citizens.

4. To foster and support activities for the moral, mental, intellectual, and physical well-being of young people in the community.

5. To found and/or provide scholarships for deserving students and for graduates or undergraduates of colleges and universities, and to assist them in attending any educational institution.

6. To carry on educational, recreational, social, and other activities aimed at the prevention and treatment of juvenile delinquency and crime.

7. To raise and disburse funds and to rent, lease, or hold property, real or personal, for purposes of and relative to such work. No part of the net earnings, if any, shall inure to the benefit of any individual member.

Article III: Membership

The membership of the corporation shall be composed of residents and former residents of the area and any other citizens, regardless of race, creed, or national origin, who are interested in furthering the objectives of the organization.

1. There shall be no limit to the number of members.

2. Members may be required to pay dues or other assessments as determined by the Board of Directors.

3. Activities, programs, and other educational and recre-

ational opportunities shall be made available to any person residing within the geographic area served by the committee, regardless of race, religion, or national origin.

4. All members shall sign an application in the form herein set out, and shall subscribe to the ideals and objectives of the committee.

CERTIFICATE OF MEMBERSHIP

_____

NAME OF COMMITTEE

I _____ have accepted membership in the committee, organized to foster and support programs for local residents through the enlisting of the efforts of our friends and neighbors.

_____   _____

Address   *Phone*

_____   _____

Date   *President's signature*

5. Meetings of the committee shall be held monthly at 7:30 P.M. and such other times as the president may direct.

6. Fifteen or more members shall compose a quorum for the transaction of business pertinent to the committee program, although any lesser number may adjourn any meeting.

ARTICLE IV: BOARD OF DIRECTORS

The business of this corporation shall be managed by a Board of Directors, and the entire program of the organization shall be subject to the counsel, guidance, and approval of this Board.

Membership on the Board of Directors shall be open to any person of good moral character, regardless of race, creed, or national origin, who is interested in furthering the objectives of the organization.

1.   The Board of Directors shall consist of (specify number) of members, elected to serve for three years and until their respective successors shall be elected and qualified. Any director may be reelected to succeed himself or herself for an unlimited number of terms.

2.   [*Designate number here: one-third of total number of directors is recommended*] directors shall be elected each year, along with replacements for other vacancies.

3.   Election of directors shall take place at the general meeting of the membership during the second week in November. Elected directors will take office at the December meeting following said election.

4.   Vacancies that occur for any reason whatsoever between the regular elections may be filled for the unexpired term by special election by the remaining directors at any regular or special meeting of the Board.

5.   The Board of Directors shall meet at least once each quarter or when requested in writing by at least five members of the Board of Directors, or at such times as the president may direct.

ARTICLE V: OFFICERS

The officers shall be members of the corporation in good standing and are as follows:

> President
> First Vice-President
> Second Vice-President
> Third Vice-President
> Secretary
> Treasurer
> Sergeant-at-Arms

1. Election of officers: The officers shall be elected annually by the members by secret ballot at the meeting held on the second Wednesday in the month of November, and shall take office at the December meeting following that election. Nominations will be made and reported to the members by the nominating committee, and may also be made from the floor at the annual election.

2. Tenure of office: Each officer shall hold office for one year or until a successor shall have been elected and qualified. A vacancy in any office shall be filled by a majority vote of the members to complete the unexpired term. (Exception: A vacancy in the office of president will be filled for the unexpired term by the first vice-president.) Any officer may be reelected to succeed himself or herself for an unlimited number of terms, except the president, who shall not be elected for more than two consecutive terms.

3. Duties of officers

   a. The duly elected president is automatically president of the Board of Directors and shall preside over all business meetings of the corporation. All that pertains to the interest of the organization shall be supervised and directed by the president, who shall sign all documents relative to the affairs of the organization as may be necessary, and who shall approve disbursements by countersigning checks for ordinary expenditures authorized by the organization whenever deemed necessary. The president shall have the power to appoint any committee that the group deems necessary at any meeting.

   b. The first vice-president shall assist the president in every way possible and preside in the absence of the president. In the event of the office of president becoming vacant for any cause, the first vice-president shall assume the office of president for the remainder of the unexpired term.

   c. The second vice-president and third vice-president shall officiate in numerical order, in the absence of the president and first vice-president, and shall perform such other duties as the president may assign them.

d. The secretary shall keep the minutes of all meetings of the organization and shall keep all records of the corporation.

e. The treasurer shall supervise the handling of funds belonging to the organization, keep proper records of same, and make all the disbursements properly authorized by the organization. Payments will be made by check signed by the treasurer and countersigned by the president.

f. The sergeant-at-arms shall maintain decorum and order at the meetings, and shall execute all orders of the president with respect to the discipline of the members.

ARTICLE VI: EXECUTIVE DIRECTOR

The board of directors is empowered to employ an executive director who will serve as agent for the corporation, assist in the planning and management of the program, and expedite the work of the committee. He is to be responsible to and under the immediate supervision of the _____ Committee.

ARTICLE VII: GENERAL PROVISIONS

1. Conduct of meetings: All meetings of this corporation shall be conducted under *Robert's Rules of Order, Revised.* The following order of business shall be pursued as nearly as possible:
Call to order
Roll call of members
Reading of minutes of last meeting
Reading of correspondence and communications
Unfinished business
Reports of officers and committees
Voting on candidates for membership
New business
Adjournment

2.   Amending the bylaws: These bylaws shall not be changed, altered, or modified except by amendment as hereinafter provided. A proposed amendment may be submitted by any member and shall be discussed at the next following regular meeting. The secretary shall give reasonable and due notice, through the mail, to all members prior to said meeting, stating therein the nature of the proposed amendment. A three-quarter vote of the members present at such a meeting shall be necessary for the adoption of the amendment.

Appendix 2

OATH FOR COMMITTEE OFFICERS

You have been elected to serve as officers of the _____
_____ Community Committee for the year
_____. You are responsible for the successful
operation of the committee, including the securing of adequate
support, the proper disbursement of funds, and the implementation of the program as formulated by the board of directors
of the _____ Community Committee in keeping
with the charter and the bylaws.

Do you accept these responsibilities and will you actively
assist your fellow officers and members in carrying out the
program of the _____ Community Com-
mittee? If so, please signify by saying, "I do."

By the authority invested in me as installing officer, I
hereby declare you duly installed in your respective offices and
take this opportunity to congratulate each of you and extend
my best wishes for a successful and rewarding year. [As these
last words are said, shake the hand of each officer. Turn to the
audience and say the following:]

Ladies and gentlemen, may I present the new officers of the
_____ Community Committee.

Appendix 3

LEGISLATION CREATING MUNICIPAL AND TOWNSHIP YOUTH COMMISSIONS

A. An Ordinance Creating the Moline Commission on Youth

BE IT ORDAINED BY THE CITY COUNCIL OF THE CITY OF MOLINE, ILLINOIS:

Section 1. There shall be created the "Moline Commission on Youth," consisting of fifteen members who are residents of the City of Moline and who over the years have shown a special, vital and public-spirited interest in youth leadership and youth problems.

Section 2. The overall purpose of said commission shall be to encourage the continuing betterment of opportunities for the wholesome development of youth in Moline.

Section 3. The members of said commission shall be appointed by the mayor, subject to approval by the city council. In making appointments, the mayor shall first consider recommendations made by the Moline Commission on Youth.

The Moline Juvenile Council shall make the initial recommendations to the mayor for appointments to the commission within thirty days after the passage and approval of this ordinance. Thereafter, in the month of March, the Moline Commission on Youth shall make its recommendations for appointments to fill terms of members expiring, which appointments shall be effective April 1. Such recommendations for special appointments to said commission shall be made as vacancies occur.

Section 4. Terms of the members of the Moline Commission on Youth shall be for three years, except for the terms of the initial appointees, which shall be assigned so that the terms of five members shall be for three years ending March 31, 1962, and five members for two years ending March 31, 1961, and five members for one year ending March 31, 1960. The fiscal year of said commission shall be April 1 to March 31.

The commission shall select its own chairman and officers in accordance with procedures which said commission may adopt.

Section 5. The Moline Commission on Youth shall:

a.   Assist in coordinating and integrating governmental and private plans and services affecting the welfare of children and youth in the city.

b.   Assist in coordinating and integrating all plans and services for protecting children from exposure to harmful influences and conditions conducive to delinquency.

c.   Make or cause to be made studies and surveys related to juvenile behavior or in the interest of youth guidance.

d.   Request and obtain such cooperation, assistance, and data from city departments and agencies as may be reasonably necessary to carry out its work.

e.   Create subcommittees, composed of members or nonmembers and assist in the work of the commission.

f.   Create a special subcommittee consisting of persons qualified by experience and training to provide guidance and counsel to children referred to it by the police department, the family court, the schools, or any social agency.

Section 6. The Moline Commission on Youth shall prepare and submit to the city council a summary report of its operations, studies, meetings held and attendance of members during the preceding fiscal year, along with a statement of projected plans for the subsequent fiscal year. The commission shall keep a written record of its proceedings, which shall be available for public inspection.

Section 7. All ordinances and parts of ordinances in conflict herewith are hereby repealed insofar as they do so conflict.

Section 8. This ordinance shall be in full force and effect from and after its passage and approval, as required by law.

———————————————————

Mayor's signature

Passed: March 10, 1959
Approved:
Attest:

———————————————————

City Clerk

B. The Evanston Youth Commission

AN ORDINANCE Creating a Youth Commission for the City of Evanston:

BE IT ORDAINED BY THE CITY COUNCIL OF THE CITY OF EVANSTON, COOK COUNTY, ILLINOIS:

Section 1. That section 2–181 of the Code of the City of Evanston, 1957, as amended, is further amended by adding thereto Sections 2–181 through 2–184, to read as follows:

Article X. Youth Commission

Section 2–181. *Creation and Appointment.* There is hereby created a Youth Commission for the City of Evanston. The Youth Commission shall consist of nine members and six nonvoting associate members to be appointed by the mayor with the advice and consent of the city council. In the appointment of said members and associate members, the mayor and city council shall give consideration to the broad representation of all groups and individuals, lay and professional, from within the social and religious structure of the community.

Section 2–184. *Powers of the Commission.* The Evanston Youth Commission shall have the following powers and duties:

a. To encourage youth of the city by publicizing and otherwise focusing attention upon accomplishments of youth groups and individuals in the city.

b. To engage in such fact-finding and studies as may be necessary to provide information about the nature and extent of Evanston's youth needs and to suggest programs necessary or desirable to promote the interest and well being of the youth of the city.

c. To cooperate with all public and private youth organizations within the community; to work with all agencies and organizations, both public and private, in the community which serve youth; to promote interagency cooperation and communication; and to promote full utilization of the existing community facilities for the benefit of the youth of the city.

d. To give consideration to unmet needs of youth and to recommend programs to the city council for meeting such needs.

e. To conduct public education and information programs to inform the community of youth accomplishments and needs.

f. To submit an annual report to the mayor and the city council on all activities of the Youth Commission, together with such recommendations as the commission shall wish to transmit.

g. With city council approval, to accept and expend contributions and gifts for programs and purposes of the commission.

Section 2: This ordinance shall be in full force and effect from and after its passage and approval in the manner provided by law.

APPROVED July 26, 1965
(Signed) JOHN D. EMERY
Mayor

PURPOSE STATEMENT CONCERNING THE EVANSTON YOUTH COMMISSION

The purpose of the Evanston Youth Commission is focused upon programs of both prevention and treatment, and its functions include the following:

1. To concern itself continuously with fact-finding and study in order to provide information about the nature and extent of our youth needs, and to suggest ways and means for remedial or preventive programs.

2. To work with all agencies and organizations both public and private in the community which serve youth, to promote cooperative efforts, and to improve inter-agency communication.

3. To give careful consideration to the needs of youth which are not being met, and to implement a program of meeting such needs by expansion, realignment, or development of new services.

4. To conduct public education and information programs, to inform the community of youth needs, to encourage and mobilize citizen interest and concern.

5. To give special and immediate attention to the development of youth centers. The commission should recommend the establishment of one major youth center (perhaps under the cooperative auspices of school, church, and recreational authorities) as well as the development of a subcenter system based on the "lighted schoolhouse" concept.

6. To support the plan for a regional juvenile court, and to lend all appropriate assistance to the establishment of this court.

7. To promote cooperation between legal and school authorities on problems relating to truancy.

To attain these ends, the Evanston Youth Commission has established the following subcommittees:

A. Community Liaison
B. Educational Services
C. Recreational Services
D. Protective and Correctional Services
E. Social Services
F. Youth Services

To accomplish the goals set forth here, the Evanston Youth Commission needs the interest and support of an alert body of citizens. Its program of education and communication is designed to insure the cooperation of the community with the commission. Only through this cooperation can the needs of Evanston's youth be met, now and in the future.

C. BYLAWS OF THE LYONS TOWNSHIP COMMITTEE ON YOUTH

Article I: Name

Section 1. The organization shall be called the Lyons Township Committee on Youth.

Article II: Authorization

Section 1. Pursuant to 126.9 of Chapter 139 of the Illinois Revised Statutes, the board of auditors of Lyons Township at its meeting held on December 30, 1974, appointed the initial members of the Township Committee on Youth.

Article III: Statutory Purposes

Section 1. The Township Committee on Youth shall cooperate with the Illinois Commission on Delinquency Prevention in developing programs designed to prevent juvenile delinquency, and may develop programs of its own to combat delinquency.

Section 2. The Illinois Commission on Delinquency Prevention or other proper authority may request the Township Committee on Youth to counsel any person in order to prevent or combat juvenile delinquency.

Section 3. The members of the Township Committee on Youth may cooperate and work in conjunction with the members of other township committees on youth.

Article IV: Members

Section 1. The number of members shall be the number appointed from time to time by the board of auditors, not to exceed the statutory limit of eleven members.

Section 2. Members shall serve without compensation, but shall be allowed necessary expenses incurred in the performance of their duties.

Section 3. After the initial appointments, the term of each member shall be three years, but the initial appointments will be either for one or two or three years for each third of the initial members, so as to create continuity in the changing membership. The terms of members shall terminate on March 1 in the year designated by their appointment.

Section 4. In the event of the death or resignation of a member, the board of auditors may appoint a successor member who shall fill the unexpired term of such deceased or resigned member. A member may resign by notice in writing given to the township supervisor or town clerk. Three consecutive unexcused absences at regularly scheduled committee meetings or a total of five absences in any one year period shall vacate an appointment and require a reappointment or replacement.

Article V: Meeting of Members

Section 1. Regular meetings of the members shall be held on such dates and at such time and place within Lyons Township as the members shall, by resolution, from time to time determine without notice other than such resolution.

Section 2. Special meetings may be called by the chairman of the committee or by two members by personal contact or by notice in writing setting forth the date, time, and place within Lyons Township and the purpose or purposes of such meeting, filed with the secretary and given to each member at least forty-eight hours prior to the time set for the meeting.

Section 3. A majority of the members then in office shall constitute a quorum for the transaction of business at any meeting. Once a quorum is established, the act of a majority of the members present at the time of the act shall be the act of the Committee on Youth at that meeting. All votes shall be by voice or by a show of hands.

Section 4. All meetings of the members shall be open to the public.

Section 5. The rules of parliamentary practice comprised in the *Roberts Rules of Order, Revised* shall govern the proceedings of the committee and its subcommittees, subject to special rules which may be adopted by the committee.

Article VI: Officers

Section 1. The officers of the Committee on Youth shall consist of a chairman, a vice chairman, a secretary, and a treasurer, each of whom shall be a member of the committee, and such other officers as the committee may from time to time elect, specifying their duties.

Section 2. The officers shall be elected annually at the first meeting of the board of auditors after the annual town meeting. Each officer shall hold office until his successor shall have been elected and shall have qualified or until his prior death, resignation, or disqualification. A vacancy in any office may be filled by the members at any regular or special meeting to hold office for the unexpired portion of the term.

Section 3. The chairman shall appoint the members of any

subcommittee established by the committee. The chairman shall perform all the duties required of the principal officer of the committee. The Nominating Committee shall be appointed by the chairman and shall consist of three members. It will be responsible for presenting candidates for the offices of chairman, vice chairman, secretary, and treasurer.

Section 4. In the absence of the chairman, the vice chairman shall perform the duties of the chairman.

Section 5. The secretary shall: (a) keep the minutes of the meetings of the members in one or more books provided for that purpose, (b) be custodian of the records of the committee, and (c) certify, when necessary, the acts of the members.

Section 6. The treasurer shall examine and approve all expenditures related to the activities of the committee before any bills are paid.

Article VII: Duties and Powers

Section 1. The committee may make rules and regulations concerning the rendition or operation of services and facilities under its direction or supervision not inconsistent with the direction of the Lyons Township Board of Auditors. It shall:

    a.   Hold meetings at least annually.

    b.   Review and evaluate community youth services.

    c.   Submit to the Township Board of Auditors a program for youth services.

    d.   Within amounts appropriated therefore, execute such programs and maintain such services and facilities as may be authorized under such appropriations.

    e.   Publish annually, within ninety days after the end of the fiscal year, for free distribution, an annual budget and report showing the condition of its trust for the year, the sums of money received from all sources, giving the name of the donor, how all monies have been expended and for what purpose, and such other statistics and program information in regard to the work of the board as it may deem to be of general interest. (The number of all employees, consultants, and other personnel shall be set forth, along with the amounts of money received.)

    f.   Consult with other local private and public agencies in the development of local plans for the most efficient delivery of youth services.

    g.   Enter into contracts for rendition or operation of services and facilities on a per capita basis or otherwise.

    h.   Employ such personnel as may be necessary to carry out the programs of the youth committee.

Article VIII: Finances

Section 1. The Committee on Youth shall operate within the committee's budget as approved and adopted by the board of auditors. A recommended committee budget shall be presented to the board of auditors not later than the date specified by the board of auditors for its receipt thereof.

Section 2. No funds shall be expended except in furtherance of a program approved by the committee.

Section 3. The fiscal year of the committee shall be the same as the fiscal year of Lyons Township.

Article IX: Amendment

These bylaws may be amended by the act of the members at any regular or special meeting with the approval thereof by the board of auditors. A copy of each such amendment, certified by the secretary, shall be filed by the secretary with the township supervisor or town clerk, and if such amendment is not acted on by the board of auditors not later than at the second meeting of the board after such filing, then it shall be deemed to have been approved by the board.

LEGISLATION CREATING THE ILLINOIS COMMISSION ON DELINQUENCY PREVENTION

PUBLIC ACT 79–944
HOUSE BILL 199

An Act creating the Illinois Commission on Delinquency Prevention, and amending the Unified Code of Corrections.

Be it enacted by the People of the State of Illinois, represented in the General Assembly:

Section 1. (S. H. A. ch. 23, #2701)

This Act shall be known and may be cited as the Illinois Commission on Delinquency Prevention Act.

Section 2. (S. H. A. ch. 23, #2702)

The purpose of this Act is to conserve the human resources represented by the youth of the State and to protect society more effectively by providing a program looking toward the prevention of delinquency and crime and by assisting communities in establishing and operating youth welfare and delinquency prevention programs designed to divert children away from the criminal justice system, and by coordinating these programs. Since conditions contributing to delinquency exist in the community where the delinquency child is raised and in the circumstances and associations which effect[1] his early development, it is, therefore, declared that the prevention of delinquency is a matter of public concern and that the State shall encourage the development of local community organizations for effective action on this problem. The enlistment of local people individually and in organized groups in cooperative efforts to attack the problem of delinquency in their immediate neighborhood shall be a basic purpose of the Commission.

Section 3. (S. H. A. ch. 23, #2703)

There is hereby created the Illinois Delinquency Prevention Commission, hereinafter referred to as the Commission.

The Commission shall consist of fifteen members appointed by the Governor with the advice and consent of the Senate. Initial appointments shall be made before December 31, 1975. Of those members first appointed, three shall serve until the third Monday of January, 1977, and until their successors are appointed and qualified, three shall serve until the third Monday of January, 1978, and until their successors are appointed and qualified, three shall serve until the third Monday in January, 1979, and until their successors are appointed and qualified, and three shall serve until the third Monday in January, 1980, and until their successors are appointed and qualified. After the original terms expire, all terms shall be for five years and until successors are appointed and qualified. Vacancies shall be filled for the unexpired term.

The Governor shall designate one member as Chairman of the Commission.

Members of the Commission shall serve without compensation but shall be reimbursed for actual and necessary expenses incurred in the performance of their duties.

All persons appointed to the Commission shall be knowledgeable in the general area of youth problems, juvenile delin-

[1]So in enrolled bill.

quency, or in planning and conducting programs for the prevention of delinquency and the treatment of delinquents.

Section 4. (S. H. A. ch. 23, #2704)

The Governor shall appoint an executive director of the Commission who shall be an ex-officio member of the Commission and shall report to the Commission as requested. The executive director shall have extensive experience in the study of delinquency, methods of treatment and prevention, and in the administration of programs for delinquency control. The Commission shall determine the salary of the executive director.

Section 5. (S. H. A. ch. 23, #2705)

The Commission has the powers and duties defined in Sections 5.1 through 5.11.

Section 5.1. (S. H. A. ch. 23, #2705.1)

To form groups of local citizens and assist these groups, through education, in conducting activities aimed at the prevention and control of juvenile delinquency, making use of local people and resources for such purposes as:

a.   Combating local conditions known to contribute to delinquency.

b.   Developing recreational and other programs for youth work.

c.   Providing adult sponsors for delinquent cases.

d.   Dealing with other related problems of the locality.

Section 5.2. (S. H. A. ch. 23, #2705.2)

To advise local, state, and federal officials and public and private agencies and lay groups on methods for the reduction and prevention of delinquency and the treatment of delinquents.

Section 5.3. (S. H. A. ch. 23, #2705.3)

To consult with the schools, police, and courts of this state on the development of programs for the reduction and prevention of delinquency and the treatment of delinquents.

Section 5.4 (S. H. A. ch. 23, #2705.4)

To cooperate with other agencies whose resources deal with the care and treatment of delinquents to the end that wherever possible they be assisted to a successful adjustment outside of institutional care.

Section 5.5. (S. H. A. ch. 23, #2705.5)

To cooperate with other agencies in surveying, developing, and utilizing the human and institutional resources of a community as a means of combatting the problem of delinquency and of effectuating rehabilitation.

Section 5.6. (S. H. A. ch. 23, #2705.6)

To hold district and state conferences from time to time in order to acquaint the public with current problems of juvenile delinquency and develop a sense of civic responsibility toward delinquency prevention.

Section 5.7. (S. H. A. ch. 23, #2705.7)

To assemble and distribute information relating to delinquency, and to report on studies relating to community conditions which affect the problem of delinquency.

Section 5.8. (S. H. A. ch. 23, #2705.8)

To assist any community within the state by conducting a comprehensive survey of the community's available resources, public and private, and recommend methods of establishing a community program for combatting juvenile delinquency and crime, but no such survey shall be conducted unless and until local individuals and groups request it through their local authorities, and no such request shall be interpreted as binding the community in following recommendations made by this Commission as a result thereof.

Section 5.9. (S. H. A. ch. 23, #2705.9)

To develop a statewide central records system for juveniles and make information available to local registered participating police youth officers so that police youth officers will be able to obtain rapid access to the juvenile's background from other jurisdictions to the end that the police youth officers can make appropriate dispositions which will best serve the interest of the child and the community.

To develop safeguards to guarantee the confidentiality of such records except when used for the following purposes:

1. For a dispositional hearing under the Juvenile Court Act.[2]
2   Inquiries from registered police officers.

For the purposes of this Act, "police youth officer" means a member of a duly organized state, county, or municipal police force who is trained and assigned by his superintendent, sheriff, or chief of police, as the case may be, to specialize in youth problems.

Section 5.10. (S. H. A. ch. 23, #2705.10)

To provide assistance through grants-in-aid or sponsorship of programs or projects designed to carry out the purpose of this Act.

Section 5.11. (S. H. A. ch. 23, #2705.11)

To consider and study the entire field of juvenile delinquency, and to advise the Governor and General Assembly.

Section 5.12. (S. H. A. ch. 23, #2705.12)

To adopt rules to carry out the purposes of this Act. Such rules shall be filed with the Governor and the General Assembly.

Section 6. (S. H. A. ch. 23, #2706)

In the performance of its powers and duties, the Commission may employ such personnel as it deems necessary, subject to the Personnel Code.[3]

Section 7. (S. H. A. ch. 23, #2707)

The Commission shall meet as prescribed in its rules, but at least once every three months. The Commission shall keep minutes of each meeting. Such minutes are public records and shall be made available for public inspection by the Commission.

The Commission shall give reasonable public notice of its meetings and shall permit public participation at such meetings.

[2]Chapter 37, #701–1 et seq.
[3]Chapter 127, #63b101 et seq.

Section 8. (S. H. A. ch. 23, #2708)

The Commission shall file an annual report of its operations with the General Assembly and the Governor before February 1 of each year.

Section 9. (S. H. A. ch. 23, #2709)

As soon as the Governor has appointed at least eight members of the Commission, all personnel, materials, records, and other resources, including grant-in-aid funds, and equipment of the Community Services Section of the Juvenile Division, Department of Corrections, and all personnel, materials, records, and equipment of the Illinois Juvenile Officers Identification File in the Bureau of Identification of the Department of Law Enforcement shall be transferred to the Delinquency Prevention Commission.

The transfer of such personnel shall not affect the status of such employees under civil service or other laws relating to State employees.

Section 10. Sections 3–15–1 of the "Unified Code of Corrections," approved July 26, 1972, as amended, is amended to read as follows:

Section 3–15–1. (S. H. A. ch. 38, #1003–15–1)

Purpose

The Department shall:

Establish and provide post release treatment programs for juvenile offenders committed to the Department and released by the Parole and Pardon Board.

Approved Sept. 11, 1975

Effective Oct. 1, 1975

Note: On July 1, 1978 the statewide central records system operated by the Commission's Juvenile Officers Information Division was transferred to the Department of Law Enforcement and the Illinois Status Offenders Service was transferred from the Department of Children and Family Services to the Commission on Delinquency Prevention.

BIBLIOGRAPHY

Abrahamson, J. *A neighborhood finds itself.* New York: Harper and Brothers, 1959.

Alinsky, S. *Reveille for radicals.* Chicago: University of Chicago Press, 1945.

Allison, A. *The principles of population and the connection with human happiness.* London: Blackwood & Son, 1840.

Beck, B. Delinquents—outcasts of society. Lecture delivered in Chicago: Welfare Council of Metropolitan Chicago, 1955.

Beck, B. Innovations in combating juvenile delinquency. *Children,* March–April 1965, 69–74.

Belass, D. W., & Ryan, E. J. Use of indigenous non-professionals in probation and parole. *Federal Probation,* March 1972, 10.

Bendix, F. A. *The effectiveness of the Area Project as a means of social control.* (Master's thesis, The University of Chicago) Chicago, 1952.

Bernstein, S. *Youth on the streets.* New York: Association Press, 1964.

Burgess, E. W. Community organization—a resource for youth. In A. Sorrentino (Ed.), *The delinquent and his neighbors.* Milburn, N.J.: R. F. Publishing, 1975.

Burgess, E. W., & Bogue, D. J. (Eds.) *Urban sociology.* Chicago: University of Chicago Press, 1967.

Carey, J. T. *Sociology and public affairs: The Chicago school.* Beverly Hills, Cal.: Sage Publications, 1975.

Cavan, R. S. *Juvenile delinquency.* Philadelphia: J. B. Lippincott, 1962.

Chicago Area Project. Chicago: 1939. (In University of Chicago Regenstein Library Card Catalog.)

Clay, J. *The prison chaplain.* London: Macmillan and Co., 1861.

Coyle, G. L. Education for social action. In J. Lieberman (Ed.), *New trends in group work.* New York: Association Press, 1938.

Cutlip, S. M. *Fund raising in the United States: The role of American philanthropy.* New Brunswick, N.J.: Rutgers University Press, 1965.

Dewey, J. *Human nature and conduct.* New York: Henry Holt, 1922.

Fellows, M. M. *Testing methods for raising money for church, health and welfare agencies.* New York: Harper, 1959.

Finestone, H. The Chicago Area Project in theory and practice. In *Community Organization.* Publications, 1972.

Finestone, H. *Victims of change: Juvenile delinquents in American society.* Westport, Conn.: Greenwood Press, 1976.

Fish, J. H. *Black power/white control.* Princeton, N.J.: Princeton University Press, 1973.

Flanagan, J. *The grass roots fund raising book: How to raise money in your community.* Chicago: Swallow Press, 1977.

Glueck, S. & Glueck, E. T. *1,000 juvenile delinquents.* New York: Harvard University Press, 1934.

Heiser, V. *An American doctor's odyssey.* New York: W. W. Norton, 1936.

Hendry, C. E. Democratizing administration. *Association Boys' Work Journal,* January 1939.

Knapp, D., & Polk, K. *Scouting the war on poverty.* Lexington, Mass.: Heath Lexington Books, 1975.

Knowles, H. K. *How groups raise funds.* Freeport, Maine: Bond Wheelwright, 1961.

Kobrin, S. The Chicago Area Project—a 25 year assessment. *The Annals of the American Academy of Political and Social Science,* March 1959, Vol. 322 19–29.

Kobrin, S. The formal logical properties of the Shaw-McKay delinquency theory. In H. L. Voss & D. M. Petersen (Eds.), *Ecology, crime and delinquency.* New York: Appleton-Century-Crofts, 1971.

Mannheim, B. *The Chicago Area Project: In theory and practice.* (Master's thesis, University of Illinois) Urbana, 1953.

Martin, J. B. A new attack on delinquency. *Harper's Magazine,* May 1944.

Martin, M. People who care. *Illinois Education Association,* May 1962, **24** (9).

McKay, H. D. The neighborhood and child conduct. *The Annals of the American Academy of Political and Social Science,* January 1949, **261,** 32–41.

McKay, H. D. Differential association and crime prevention: Problems of utilization. *Social Problems,* Summer 1960, **8,** 25–38.

McKay, H. D. Social influence on adolescent behavior. *The Journal of the American Medical Association,* November 10, 1962, **182,** 643–649.

McKay, H. D. *Report on the criminal careers of male delinquents in Chicago.* Task Force Report: Juvenile Delinquency and Youth Crime. The President's Commission on Law Enforcement and Administration of Justice. U.S. Government Printing Office, Washington, D.C.: 1967, 107–114.

McKay, H. D. *Subsequent arrests, convictions, and commitments among former juvenile delinquents.* The President's Commission on Law Enforcement and Administration of Justice, 1967.

Merritt, I. Up from charity—an experiment in neighborhood organization. In Joshua Lieberman (Ed.), *New trends in group work.* New York: Association Press 1938, pp. 28–46.

North, C. C. *The community and social welfare.* New York: McGraw-Hill, 1931.

Park, R. E., Burgess, E. W. & McKenzie, R. D. *The city.* Chicago: University of Chicago Press, 1935.

Plant, J. S. *Personality and the cultural pattern.* New York: Commonwealth Fund, 1937.

Pritchard, J. H. *Complete fund earning guide.* New York: A. J. L. Publishing, 1967.

Rice, S. A. Hypothesis and verification in Clifford R. Shaw's studies of juvenile delinquency. In S. A. Rice (Ed.), *Methods in social science.* Chicago: University of Chicago Press, 1931.

Shaw, C. R. *The natural history of a delinquent career.* Chicago: University of Chicago Press, 1931.

Shaw, C. R. Neighborhood program for the treatment of delinquency. *Quarterly of the Minnesota Education, Philanthropic, Correctional and Penal Institutions,* September 1933, **33.**

Shaw, C. R. The Chicago Area Project. In W. C. Reckless (Ed.), *Criminal behavior.* New York: McGraw-Hill, 1940.

Shaw, C. R. Methods, accomplishments and problems of the Chicago Area Project. Mimeographed Report, 1944.

Shaw, C. R. *The jack-roller.* (Rev. ed.) Chicago: University of Chicago Press, 1966.

Shaw, C. R., Burgess, E. W., & Lohman, J. D. The Chicago Area Project. In *Coping with crime.* New York: Year Book of the National Probation Association, 1937.

Shaw, C. R., & Jacobs, J. A. The Chicago Area Project: An experimental community program for the prevention of delinquency in Chicago. In *Proceedings of the 69th annual conference of the American Prison Association.* New York: 1939.

Shaw, C. R., & McKay, H. D. *Juvenile delinquency and urban areas.* Chicago: University of Chicago Press, (Rev. ed.) 1969.

Shaw, C. R., & McKay, H. D. *Social factors in delinquency.* No. 13, Vol. II, Report on the Causes of Crime. National Commission on Law Observance and Enforcement. Washington, D.C.: U.S. Government Printing Office, 1931.

Shaw, C. R., McKay, H. D., & McDonald, J. F. *Brothers in crime.* Chicago: University of Chicago Press, 1938.

Shaw, C. R., & Sorrentino, A. Is gang busting wise? *National Parent Teacher,* January 1956, Vol. L. No. 5, 18–20.

Shaw, C. R., Zorbaugh, F. M., McKay, H. D. & Cottrell, L. D. *Delinquency areas.* Chicago: University of Chicago Press, 1929.

Sherman, R. D. *The west side community committees: A people's organization in action.* (Master's thesis, University of Chicago) Chicago, 1946.

Short, J. F. Introduction in Clifford R. Shaw and Henry D. McKay, *Juvenile delinquency and urban areas.* Chicago: University of Chicago Press, 1969.

Short, J. F. (Ed.) *Delinquency, crime and society.* Chicago: University of Chicago Press, 1976.

Snodgrass, J. *The American criminological tradition: Portraits of the men and ideology in a discipline.* (Doctoral dissertation, University of Pennsylvania) Philadelphia, 1972.

Snodgrass, J. Clifford Shaw and Henry McKay: Chicago criminologists. *British Journal of Criminology,* January 1976, Vol. 16, No. 1, pp. 1–19.

Sorrentino, A. The Chicago Area Project after 25 years. *Federal Probation,* June 1959, **23,** 40–45.

Sorrentino, A. Cultural aspects of violent and disturbed youth. In *Proceedings of the ninetieth annual congress of correction.* New York: American Correctional Congress, August 1960.

Sorrentino, A. (Ed.) The Chicago Area Project after 40 years. In *The delinquent and his neighbors.* Milburn, N.J.: R. F. Publishing, 1975.

Sorrentino, A. *Organizing against crime: Redeveloping the neighborhood.* New York: Human Sciences Press, 1977.

South Side Community Committee. *Bright shadows in bronzetown.* Chicago: South Side Community Committee, 1949.

Spergel, I. A. *Community problem solving: The delinquency example.* Chicago: University of Chicago Press, 1969.

Spergel, I. A. (Ed.) *Community organization: Studies in constraint.* Beverly Hills, Cal.: Sage Publications, 1972.

Sullivan, H. S. Physical and cultural environment. In *The gist of it: Summary and conclusions of the symposium on mental health.* Section on Medical Sciences, American Association for the Advancement of Science. Richmond, Va., 1938.

Taylor, H. B. The Chicago Area Project as seen by a social worker. Unpublished document, Chicago Historical Society, 1935. (a)

Taylor, H. B. Report on the investigation of the Area Project. Unpublished document, Chicago Historical Society, 1935. (b)

Thomas, W. I., & Znaniecki, F. *The Polish peasant in Europe and America.* New York: A. Knopf, 1927.

Tunley, R. *Kids, crime and chaos.* New York: Harper and Brothers, 1962.

Waldron, R. J., Uppal, G., Quarles, C. L., McCauley, R. P., Harper, H., Frazier, R. L., Benson, J. C., & Altemose, J. R. *The criminal justice system: An introduction.* Boston: Houghton Mifflin, 1976.

Ware, C. F. *Greenwich Village 1920–1930: A comment on American civilization in the post-war years.* Boston: Houghton Mifflin, 1935.

Witmer, H. L., & Tufts, E. *The effectiveness of delinquency prevention programs,* Children's Bureau Publication No. 350. Washington, D.C.: U.S. Department of Health, Education and Welfare, 1954.

Collections of documents on the Chicago Area Project are also available at the Chicago Historical Society and at Sangamon State University, Springfield, Ill.

INDEX